Living in
TWO
WORLDS

of related interest

Understanding Sensory Dysfunction
Learning, Development and Sensory Dysfunction in Autism Spectrum
Disorders, ADHD, Learning Disabilities and Bipolar Disorder
Polly Godwin Emmons and Liz McKendry Anderson
ISBN 978 1 84310 806 1
eISBN 978 1 84642 150 1

Ketchup is My Favorite Vegetable
A Family Grows Up with Autism
Liane Kupferberg Carter
ISBN 978 1 84905 715 8
eISBN 978 1 78450 209 6

What Color is Monday?
How Autism Changed One Family for the Better
Carrie Cariello
ISBN 978 1 84905 727 1
eISBN 978 1 78450 094 8

The Autism Discussion Page on Anxiety, Behavior, School, and
Parenting Strategies
A Toolbox for Helping Children with Autism
Feel Safe, Accepted, and Competent
Bill Nason
ISBN 978 1 84905 995 4
eISBN 978 0 85700 943 2

Pretending to be Normal
Living with Asperger's Syndrome (Autism Spectrum Disorder)
Expanded Edition
Liane Holliday Willey
ISBN 978 1 84905 755 4
eISBN 978 0 85700 987 6

Living in
TWO
WORLDS

On Being a Social Chameleon
with Asperger's

DYLAN EMMONS

Jessica Kingsley *Publishers*
London and Philadelphia

First published in 2016
by Jessica Kingsley Publishers
73 Collier Street
London N1 9BE, UK
and
400 Market Street, Suite 400
Philadelphia, PA 19106, USA

www.jkp.com

Library of Congress Cataloging in Publication Data
Names: Emmons, Dylan, author.
Title: Living in two worlds : on being a social chameleon with Asperger's /
   Dylan Emmons.
Description: London ; Philadelphia : Jessica Kingsley Publishers, 2016. |
   Includes bibliographical references.
Identifiers: LCCN 2015041430 (print) | LCCN 2015046577 (ebook) | ISBN
   9781785927065 (alk. paper) | ISBN 9781784502638 ()
Subjects: LCSH: Emmons, Dylan--Health. | Asperger's
   syndrome--Patients--Biography. | Asperger's syndrome--Social aspects.
Classification: LCC RC553.A88 E46 2016 (print) | LCC RC553.A88 (ebook) |
   DDC
   616.85/8832--dc23
LC record available at http://lccn.loc.gov/2015041430

British Library Cataloguing in Publication Data
A CIP catalogue record for this book is available from the British Library

ISBN 978 1 78592 706 5
eISBN 978 1 78450 263 8

Printed and bound in the United States

Dedicated to everyone living on the spectrum,
with sincerest gratitude to those who love,
teach, or care for someone with autism.

ACKNOWLEDGEMENTS

First and foremost, I am in debt to my best and untiring supporters: my sister, Laura; my mother, Polly; my father, Dale; and my grandmother, Frances whose belief in my writing was absolute.

I give heartfelt thanks to all of the professors at Sarah Lawrence College and Ithaca College who have helped me to develop my writing, especially Jo Ann Beard, Vijay Seshadri, Tom Kerr, Fred Wilcox, Nick Kowalczyk, Catherine Taylor, and Diane McPherson.

This work was made possible by my fellow writers, who have been my first readers and who have not only provided expert feedback on included materials, but have intimidated and inspired me with the quality of their work.

I am grateful to the teachers, aides, paraprofessionals, therapists, and bus drivers who have worked with my peers and me over the years and who are working now to enrich the lives of the students who most need it.

Special thanks to all of my friends for your continued love and encouragement, especially Jordan W.

With deepest gratitude to the memory of those who through their support and guidance at key moments in my life made this book possible, but who are no longer with us, namely Eileen O'Neil, and Dr. David Bosnick.

CONTENTS

PREFACE

A friend of mine, someone I've only become close with over the past couple of years, recently told me: "I don't think you have Asperger's; I think it's all in your head." Immediately, memories raced up to meet this statement, to disprove it: memories of conversations I've tried to have, of the countless times I've come to my senses in the middle of a conversation only to realize I was interrupting, or standing too close, or rattling on in detail about something only I am interested in. They are memories of losing myself in the world of language, of words and stories coming to me by the page, of picking up on subtle vocal inflections, of remembering thousands of useless factoids but forgetting my jacket; they're memories of meltdowns, anxieties, and rages brought on by bee stings, forgotten homework, and other minor, malicious changes in routine; they're memories of standing out, of being bullied and not knowing it, and of finding confidence and comradery in spite of or because of it all.

But memories aren't words, and in the moment, I had no means of translating such experiences into a coherent response—no adequate way to, in one or two sentences, encapsulate for my friend an adolescence full of its own idiosyncratic challenges. I could only smile and shrug. I must admit I have some mixed feelings about anyone doubting my diagnosis, especially as someone who has spent the greater part of his formative years trying to pass for "normal." And by "normal" I don't mean a fantastic, homogeneous, or utopian normal—just the license that appears to accompany a person's association with the word and that would seemingly allow me to functionally pass through the world without immediately and involuntarily highlighting my differences or eccentricities. Because most people if they met me today wouldn't know I have Asperger's Syndrome unless

I told them, the idea that I might be mistaken or even lying about having an autism spectrum disorder is a compliment and an accusation rolled into one.

Asperger's is a liminal disorder—it's a disorder of thin veils and blurry borders, of seeing people and their intentions as if through an opaque curtain. It's a disorder characterized by the accomplishments and setbacks of life on the edge of normal. Normalcy is never fully within reach, because like enlightenment or the perfect relationship, its very existence is dubious. For me and for many on the autism spectrum, some sense of normalcy has been worth chasing. And it's in the chase that one begins, however slowly, to incorporate some of its characteristics.

At this point, I suppose I've assumed enough of these characteristics so that some facts of my life do seem to stand in contrast with the picture many have of someone classified as "disabled." Now an adjunct professor in my mid-twenties, if you happened across me working at the tutoring center, writing in a café, going through my ritual at the gym, ordering a sandwich, or floundering through a first date, there'd be almost no indication of the unique struggles I've faced or how much work I've put in to reach this level of functionality. I'm both proud of and troubled by this.

Admittedly, in my everyday life, I now make use of and am thankful for the comparatively more subtle way my disorder presents itself. Also admittedly, the general public increasingly knows more about autism and is increasingly affected by it. After the advances of the past few years in technology and communication, and after so many stories, movies, and TV shows highlighting the socially awkward, even those who aren't so much "in the know" about autism are more ready to accept the characteristics of someone on the spectrum. But we're not there yet. As a group we may share many common traits, and yet everyone with a diagnosis of Asperger's and of high-functioning autism is as different from one another as we are from those not on the autism spectrum at all. So the ins and outs of the human experience on the autism spectrum remain mysterious to too many. To some, if you aren't classically, immediately, identifiably "Rain Man-autistic," you must be normal.

Of those who warmly accuse me of being normal, most, like my friend, weren't there to watch as I learned the rules of social interaction the hard way, or came to terms with a sensory system that refuses to process pain, hunger, or sound in a conventional way. Besides, the fact is that some of my childhood struggles do remain: I occasionally avoid eye contact or appear to have momentarily lost track of what my limbs are doing; I have certain areas of interest into which I pour most of my attention; I don't seem to get cold quite the same way other people do; I shut down if I'm pulled into more than one conversation; I second-guess myself when it comes to the meaning of non-verbal cues; and though my presence of mind has gotten better with time, my tendency towards forgetfulness and the nature of my profession mean that I am quite literally an absent-minded professor.

It can be said of life that it's a long process of slowly waking up, of coming to awareness about one's situation and surroundings and adapting to them. That is all I have done, and it is that unique and personal process which is detailed in this book. The adaptations that I've made from my most embarrassing moments have meant all of the difference in paving the way for my proudest accomplishments. In fact, it could be said that in a round-about way, this ability to adapt and to blend in is responsible for me writing this book, as are assertions by people I've met recently and those I've known for some time about my status as someone who's disabled. All of these moments of major and minor misunderstanding I've had—as in the above exchange with my friend, when all of those untranslatable experiences bubble up to the surface of my mind—remind me of the mutual frustration of travelers who don't share a language, of struggling to describe to another the striking and cryptic personal significance of a jarring dream. Now that I am by appearance a functioning member of society, I'm afraid the story of how I got here might slip away deeper into uncertainty of events past. I still worry that I'll eventually come to believe I've always been this way and that those feelings I remember of striving desperately for confidence or acceptance must be overdramatized or untrue. This concern would have been occasion enough for me as a compulsive writer to attempt to write my life through age eighteen. But I had a better reason.

My own missed connections and disastrous conversations with non-disabled or neuro-normative people have fascinated and haunted me. However, I can't help but notice similar scenarios playing out around me, in the lives of those classified as on and off the spectrum. And as a resident of the border between those realms, I feel compelled to do some ambassador's work. Although I can't claim to represent the "general" Asperger's experience—because such a thing does not exist—what I can offer is a perspective that many can relate to but whose challenges with articulation prevent a deeper, more gratifying understanding with those around them. So many people on the autism spectrum are now going through the same processes of becoming an individual and of integrating into society that I went through. They and their loved ones grapple daily with the disorder's limitations and to accept its opportunities. They're fascinated and haunted by this feeling they have of existing in two worlds— one internal, experiential, and intricate, the other shared. They have trouble critically analyzing and participating in the shared world at the same time. They have trouble expressing themselves in the moment and otherwise. They're aware of their isolation in the midst of a crowd, and they want to do something about it. They learn to walk around in and interact so well with the neuro-normative world that they slip right into the flow of it, standing out, in some cases, no more than anyone else, complete with his or her own quirks.

PART 1

EARLY LIFE/ ELEMENTARY SCHOOL

CHAPTER 1

THE DIAGNOSIS

It is the end of the day, and I am on a crowded bus on the way home from kindergarten. The usual bus driver, who usually tells me I am her good, quiet boy, is not here today and so we have a substitute. He's shifting around in his seat, trying to figure out where we all live. I hope he doesn't forget my stop. The normal bus driver forgot once, and Mom came sprinting down the street after her. She hasn't forgotten again, but I remind her every day anyway. The bus is extra noisy today, and the bus driver keeps yelling for everyone to quiet down.

Adam, who put glue on his tongue earlier today, is sitting near me, and the new bus driver has asked him where he lives, but because of the noise he either can't hear Adam's answer or Adam hasn't given one. As the noise mounts and the threats from the bus driver get louder and meaner, I start to beg Adam to tell the driver where he lives. Adam is not supposed to be on the bus still. He tells me "okay" but then does nothing. By now, the other kids' chattering and taunting are making me uncomfortable, like I can't sit still, like my insides can't sit still, and I want to scream and I want to move but I want to sit still because I am the bus driver's good quiet boy and I'm not part of the problem, I'm not… And then John, sitting next to me, starts to annoy me. He likes to laugh at me and make fun of me. Finally, it is enough and I take the back of his head and slam it into the seat in front of us, which gives a thud as John's head collides with it. He starts to cry. His glasses had hit his face. The bus driver asks why he's crying. I can't take this anymore. My stop is coming up, and I get off, but the bus stays parked near my house. The kids are all getting transferred to a different bus, Mom says, because the other driver does not know the stops and is having trouble. Even though I am home, it will be a while before I calm down. The noise and the pressure are gone, but their feelings fade slowly.

THE TWO CHARACTERS OF DYLAN EMMONS

My mom and I are giving a workshop on "Growing up with Asperger's Syndrome" in a small town named Jasper in upstate New York. And I think if the towns themselves could talk, they'd say they feel a lot like I did growing up: they exist on the outside; people don't quite know what to think of them. In this case, the town's mayor himself delivered the fourteen pizzas served before the presentation. It has been my experience that it's the parents and teachers in small towns that show the most interest in and appreciation for the advice and stories we have to give; here in Jasper, we'll have our largest audience to date.

I like to sit and eat with everyone before they know I'm presenting. Some entire families come; mom, dad, a baby, a toddler, and a school age boy or girl all sit down and eat. The school, like the school we visited last, has set up a child care system where students gained community service hours for watching the small children whose parents would be in my audience. I know people wouldn't be here on a school night if they didn't work with or care for an individual on the spectrum. I wonder who they've left at home.

A woman comes in, her son close behind. His hair is spiked in the front and he wears glasses. As they place their coats on the back of small chairs, she must convince the boy to give up the book he's had clutched close probably since long before their arrival. *Titanic*, it reads. I smile, thinking of another little boy on a long-ago car ride enveloped in his *Batman Forever* picture book. The kid relinquishes his book in favor of a couple of slices.

The *Titanic* kid is still on my mind as Mom and I introduce ourselves: an Ithaca College junior with Asperger's, and a high school special-education teacher and parent, here to tell our story and answer some questions. While my mom talks, I try to get a sense of the crowd, but they're difficult for me to read at first, especially now that I'm up here. It's sort of like reading the first few pages of a book—the audience and narrator getting a feel for each other.

As I begin, I have two characters to introduce. I explain that I have a mild form of autism, and that I know that no matter how hard I worked at overcoming the obstacles life with the disorder provided, a life on the spectrum will always color who I am. I identify more as a student (now a professor) and as a writer, and I would identify this as a major defining aspect of the first character I introduce to my audience. This is a persona shaped by my accumulated trials and errors interacting and integrating with what I sometimes call the shared world—the collective social sphere of relationships and chance encounters. I often wondered at the success everyone around me had with communication, and I assumed as a young child that it must rest on some quasi-supernatural ability to read minds. This persona is tasked with not only reining in the more alarming personality traits (lacking for example an "indoor voice," or tending to have extreme reactions to change or failure), but also making use of the unique resources and perspectives provided by the disorder that also accounts for my deficits. While my love for language has earned me some laughs, quizzical looks, and, thankfully, many like-minded friends, writing is a bridge out of my own world. I start by reading one of my poems, and I use it as a segue introducing my second character—the one making sense of a life on the spectrum and described, somewhat appropriately, to be off in his own world.

I read the anecdote of my kindergarten self on the bus, the losing of myself in a wave of sensory terror, the complete and utter shock of existing outside of routine. The bus ride started out all wrong, with the wrong driver who I couldn't be sure would remember my stop. The noise made it so much worse. How would the usual bus driver know I was being quiet, and therefore not part of the problem, when she heard the next day? Would I be in trouble? When I am in an environment with chaotic noise—especially conversation or repetitive noises such as alarms, wailing children, or yipping terriers—the noise begins to crowd out my logical thoughts. After a short while on the loud bus, I literally couldn't hear myself think.

There's a weird silence as I step down from the podium. Is it a confused or a knowing silence? Are they starting to see the vast gulfs between the boy I was and the man I became?

My mom stands five foot three at the podium. She has black hair tinged with gray. Behind her glasses, her blue eyes show a calm determination, and I might be the only one in the room that can see she's a little nervous. Her cheeks are slightly redder, the way they only got when she told my younger sister Laura or me to pick up after ourselves or quit arguing too many times. She's already taken off her jacket and made a joke about having hot flashes—I think it's as much to calm herself as to put the audience at ease. She shifts her feet slightly.

The screen shows a toddler in a red cap holding a can of soda, his eyes wide, peeking out of his too-large head.

"When Dylan was young, I used to feel like I was literally going crazy. For one thing, he wouldn't sleep! He didn't sleep more than forty minutes at a time until he was well into his third year. 'It just seems like that,' people told me. But you know your child. And from an early age, I knew that there was something not right. For instance, a lot of reliable sources will tell you to swaddle your kids to calm them down, and Dylan *hated* to be swaddled."

She goes on to say how confusing it was to try to play the detective with me.

"I'll admit it: one day after weeks of tantrums and neither of us sleeping, I had had enough. I left Dylan on a blanket in a onesie on the floor of our drafty apartment, and I walked into the other room. Mother of the year award, just give it to me now. But I walked back into the living room and lo and behold, he'd stopped crying!"

A cuddly youth, I preferred a cold floor to a warm embrace. I spoke early and knew and could recognize my colors, shapes, letters, and numbers up to thirty by the time I was seventeen months old. But I couldn't dress myself until well into my fourth year. My sister Laura could draw and write at age three, but I still catch myself holding my pen like a tennis racket. There's a home video of the day my younger sister and I learned how to ride bikes without training wheels, back when my parents worked on things together, when they called each other "hon." Laura rides off almost right away and I scream, wondering why my body won't let me follow.

"He got physical, occupational, and speech therapy multiple times a week from the age of three. His sister loved it—she got to play on swings, and color, etc. But Dylan hated it. The only way to get him to keep going was through constant incentive…"

STAYING IN THE LINES

A book of mazes almost as big as the table sits in front of me. Just when I think I'm getting used to mazes, we get to the next page and the lines are thinner. Sometimes it makes me want to keep going, sometimes I want to throw the book across the room. I'll be in my twenties and still reprimanding inanimate objects for slipping out of my grasp or being lost. The difference is that then, I'll do it in private, thinking even as I'm screaming how embarrassing it would be if someone in the next room were to hear.

Eileen, my occupational therapist, watches me closely and tells me when I'm not holding the pen right and reminds me all of the time to stay in the lines. She is petite and blonde, and though she won't let me forget that I am supposed to be doing my best, there is only kindness in her voice. Even with her reminding me, it's hard to remember that doing my best is all that I can do when we're working on my hands. Corners are hard, and I can't always stay inside the lines. I try not to let on that my fingers are really starting to hurt, a habit I'll keep for years, writing or typing through unbelievable cramps. Working with my hands, I think of a poem I wrote (or rather, dictated) when I had just turned five, wishing my hands were eagles' claws so that they'd be my friends. But my hands are not my friends; they don't listen to me. I'm almost at the end of the maze when one of my fingers twitches and my pencil's perfect path leaps outside of the lines. I let the pencil fall from my hands. The tip cracks and the pencil falls to the ground. My best tiger growl comes out and I fold my arms over my chest.

I'm waiting for Eileen to tell me "no animal noises," or that I'm not a tiger, but she surprises me.

"One more maze, Dylan, and then we're done. You can do that can't you? I know it's been a lot of hard work today, so what do you say if you do this next maze with me? We'll do some swings, and then we'll go down to the gift shop for some M&Ms?"

"Okay," I relent. Eileen takes me to get candy on most Fridays, but I'm surprised that she is today, too. I thought both she and Mom were mad at me.

We were in the waiting room waiting to see Eileen and I was wondering where she was—she was already three minutes late. All of a sudden, I saw someone coming in from down the hall. There was something pretty funny about this man. Did Mom or Laura see this man? Did they see how big he was? They weren't saying anything if they did. So, just as Eileen came through the door, I pointed.

"Mom, that man's morbidly obese!"

But the man left quickly, looking red.

"Why did you say that?"

"Because it's true," I said.

Later today, Mom will explain to me that I can't always say what is on my mind, especially if it has to do with someone's physical appearance. The new rule is that I don't say anything about someone's physical appearance unless I check with her or Daddy first. I won't understand now about hurt feelings—what's true about someone shouldn't hurt their feelings—but years later, I'll feel plenty of regret.

Now we're going over to the swing. Laura really likes the swings, but I don't like most of them. They make me sore. But Eileen says I'm almost done. Laura is sitting over by Mom, coloring.

"Dylan, now let's hook up the swing; come over here."

I wish I were playing Batman with Laura like I did yesterday after I got home. It made me feel better after what happened on the bus. I pretend I'm Batman and Laura pretends she's Robin, and we make up ways to fight the bad guys, like on TV. I like to plan out the fights in my head and then explain it to Laura so we can play them. But I don't like it when she doesn't do things the right way. If the Joker and his henchmen came in here, Bruce Wayne would find somewhere to turn into Batman first, but if they did he'd get Robin and use his gadgets and Karate to get them all. Sock! Bang! Boom!

"Dylan, stop talking and pay attention to me now. Now, I'm going to help you climb into the swing and we'll be done..."

SOMETHING AMISS

At around eighteen months old, I needed new shoes. So, my mom took my month-old sister and me to the store for the first of what would be many frustrating outings in search of footwear that would fit my duck feet and still look moderately cool. For a long time, my mom had to explain wherever we went, with whomever we spoke, that there were certain things I couldn't handle, that I had certain preferences. She warned the poor fellow working the kid's section that day that I didn't like to have my feet touched. The clerk assured her that he was experienced in working with kids. When the man went to touch my foot, I screamed. And I didn't just scream as if I were startled or even scared—I screamed bloody murder. I screamed until the store was empty and the mall security officers had abandoned their posts to come see what the matter was.

There were plenty of other warning signs that there was something lacking in or unusual about my development, some of which I remember and some of which I don't. I remember not wanting to eat anything except for liverwurst, blueberry muffins, and hot dogs; it was the crunchy or combative texture rather than the taste of all other foods that got to me. I don't remember not being able to hold utensils correctly well through third grade, or biting my fingers all of the time. I remember having goose eggs on my head, but I don't remember my pediatrician telling my mom to let me keep hitting my head on things—I'd eventually hurt myself and learn to stop. I do remember smacking my friend Chrissy in the head with a plastic golf club and wondering why she was upset—I'd been hitting myself in the head with it and it hadn't hurt me. I remember enjoying the book *How Animals Communicate* and a couple of other books about construction vehicles and such, but I don't remember wanting to hear them over and over again for weeks at a time. I remember having difficulty getting along with the kids in preschool, but I don't remember hitting one of them. I remember the physical effect of the Beatles' "I Will," which is the only lullaby that ever worked on me. I remember asking to hear Queen's "We Will Rock You" and "Minute by Minute" by the Doobie Brothers on repeat and singing them a capella ad infinitum. I remember the ease and gentleness with which those songs penetrated into my reinforced private sphere. But I had no idea of the potential music would hold for me as a facilitator of shared experience, and don't remember when music stepped outside of the boundaries of its own definition, becoming almost a filter through which I experienced the world. I remember the hybrid Kung Fu- and Batman-based role-playing games I played with Laura.

After two years of physical and occupational therapy and several diagnoses ranging in inaccuracy, it was time to definitively figure out what was behind my behaviors and mannerisms. For some reason, I think the story of my diagnosis is one that my mom enjoys telling most. I'll admit that I enjoy hearing the story from where I currently stand. It's a little like climbing a hill and looking back every once in a while to remember how far you've come so that you have the motivation for the rest of the insane trek. It's a good ol' stroke to the ego that will be bruised as soon as I see others sprinting past me, chatting as I wheeze.

"We went to New York City to see Isabelle Rapin, who was even then a world renowned diagnostician. I honestly didn't know what to expect; something clearly wasn't right with Dylan, but he was so smart that it was difficult to judge. On a July morning we crossed the Tappan Zee Bridge…"

"CLASSIC ASPERGER'S"

Why are we stopped? I keep asking Mom what's wrong, but all she knows is that the car isn't working. We're on the middle of a huge bridge high above water and cars whoosh past us. This is a strange place; cars aren't supposed to stop in the middle of a bridge. What if something is really wrong with the van? What if it doesn't start and we get stuck here and I have to listen to these cars honking and whizzing past? It won't be until one night when my dad and I get temporarily lost in a dark and rural part of Cape Cod (still several years before the age of ubiquitous GPS systems) that I'll begin to accept the inevitability of getting temporarily lost or inconvenienced. Dad will make it clear—in one of the only instances that a parent's yelling will ever end up calming me down—that in order for him to read the map and figure out where to go, I have to first stop perseverating.

Across the bridge there are buildings as far as my eye can see. I've never been to New York City before, never been to a place this big, and I don't know if Mom has either, but the thought that she might know her way around does not give me any comfort. The hood is up. I don't want to sit in here anymore; sitting in here won't get me any closer to the doctor, and we already came a long way to get here.

"We're going to miss the appointment!"

"Sit back and take a few deep breaths and I'm sure we'll make it to Dr. Rapin's in plenty of time."

I try to sit back, but my breaths are fast, not deep. This isn't what was supposed to happen. This isn't where I should be. What will we do if we get there too late? Even if we get off of this bridge…

"We don't know where Dr. Rapin's office is! How are we going to get there in time? We're not going to make it."

The next thing I remember is a big room full of toys and an older-looking lady. To my disbelief, we had made it to the appointment in time and I felt a lot better. Dr. Rapin asked me questions, watched me play, and I remember wondering what she was trying to figure out.

When she was done observing and I was out of the room, Dr. Rapin turned to Mom with a few sentences Mom will never forget.

"Dylan is classic Asperger's," she said, and then the next question, which caught Mom completely off guard, was how far away did we live? She was disappointed to hear that we lived almost four hours away, because Dylan was such a classic case that she'd have loved to bring him in once a month for the benefit of her students.

I imagine I can feel the lump in my mother's throat, the leathery wings of uncertainty beating at her from deep in her stomach right before she asks the question that would have been on any parent's mind.

I imagine I can hear the silence in the room, see Dr. Rapin licking her lips before she gives the opinion, in a voice not completely cold or scientific.

"I am guardedly hopeful that Dylan will lead a semi-independent life as an adult, but that remains to be seen."

CHAPTER 2

THE CLASSROOM

It's often said that higher-functioning autistic people can appear arrogant. Talking incessantly about ourselves and our own areas of interest is a talent most of us have. Part of what I'd like to call my sort of metamorphosis involves striving for reciprocal conversations and at the very least feigning interest in what someone else has to say. But I will say with a certain amount of pride that not all of us have the correct mixture of arrogance and discipline to sit and write an autobiography. So, I'll let you be the judge.

The only time that I have heard my friends say with some degree of sincerity that I am vain is when I'm around a mirror. I can't walk past a reflective surface without at least glancing into it with wonder. On some level, I think that by scrutinizing myself in windows and mirrors I'm simply overcompensating for not being able to keep my own behaviors in check as well as others. But I've always loved making faces at myself. Much to my sister's embarrassment and confusion, I've been on a life-long quest to see just how far my face can stretch in every direction and to think up characters and voices for the faces. Largely to avoid my grimacing into store windows and terrifying unsuspecting customers, Mom used to set aside a designated fifteen minutes after school for me to sit alone in front of a full length mirror and go nuts.

But as I've gotten older, the conversations between me and mirror-me have evolved a bit. I ask myself questions, taking this acceptable avenue back to the confines of my own private world. I'll give myself a look that asks, "If I saw myself walking down the street, what would I think?" Sometimes, I listen, hearing voices from the past that have embedded themselves in my own.

"When I first saw you, I was like, 'This kid's smart, what the heck's wrong with this kid?'" my substitute aid asks, back in sixth grade.

"Why does Mr. Noel follow you around?" a classmate probes a year or two later.

"If you really *do* have Asperger's..." my dad begins skeptically before he starts backpedaling. We are walking into a grocery store, and the statement catches me off guard. Of course, people have had trouble believing this about me. Usually I take it as a compliment. I will talk to him about this later and he will assure me he didn't really doubt I had it.

"I *do* have Asperger's syndrome," I have to remind myself sometimes. I let it sink in for a bit. Staring myself down, the thought seems both true and untrue. Since I'm the one living in this body, experiencing reality from the perspective of my own five senses, it's been nearly impossible to track the flow of my progress. As someone who orients himself almost obsessively according to surroundings and agenda, I admit this is unnerving. But despite the fact that I can't track it, I move towards progress. I've got a restless air about me, a young river who's working over eons to ebb away at my banks and straighten myself out at the bends.

Despite the ambiguity of how I view myself, there are times when I do feel distinctly autistic. This happens when I feel my sensory system lying to me, my ability to read situations failing. Sometimes, after an awkward silence, someone has to say "I'm *joking*" and then I'll either pretend to have known all along, or simply give them a nod that says "ahh, gotcha." Once in a while, I'll walk past some poor soul trying to hide from the wind in a huge jacket and remember, in my t-shirt, that I should be feeling cold. More often than I'd like to admit, I'll make a reference in conversation (or, worse, in class) that only I can trace back to what people were talking about in the first place.

Though I often can't decide which odd habits to attribute to basic human weirdness and which to tack up to my Asperger's, I know that autism is a part of me that always has and always will color who I am. I am usually mildly conscious of having slightly different struggles, concerns, and worries from the people I pass on the street. But in my eyes, people are not the strange race of aliens they once were; I can relate to them on some level. I can now call myself a functioning beginner in the art of small talk, and that means a lot for someone who as an eleven-year-old thought that the Beach Boys, an early obsession and precursor to my life-long affinity for music, were an appropriate conversation piece for almost any situation.

I'm pretty sure inability to decide the extent of my disability is due more to an overactive questioning gland than a lack of information. I have known I've had Asperger's for as long as I can remember.

WELCOME ANSWERS/THE ROAD AHEAD

It has been a few days since we went down to see Dr. Rapin. We are sitting in the living room, which remained dark even in the middle of the day and despite Mom's best efforts. She looks very concerned, and I want to know what's wrong.

"Dylan I want to tell you what Dr. Rapin told me..." she begins. She'll go on to say that I have Asperger's syndrome. At first, she misreads the dazed look on my face. She thinks I'm distraught, but actually a lot of loose ends are tying themselves up in my mind. *This* is why I have trouble with my hands. *This* is why I say the wrong thing sometimes, why I interrupt and don't realize why people are mad. *This* is why I'll think everyone else is as impressed as I am about how tall I look for my age. *This* is why I will have much more trouble than my younger sister when it comes time to take my training wheels off of my bike. *This* explains all of those times I couldn't keep quiet on the bus. *This* explains why I didn't understand that telling Brittany in front of everyone that she was the prettiest girl in class might embarrass her.

"Dylan?"

But I'm smiling.

"So, it isn't because I'm a bad boy!"

Mom will wrack her brain for the source of this sentiment, attempting to examine everything she's said to me. She'll eventually realize it's nothing she or Dad has said, and hopefully nothing that I heard at school (although that's not entirely unlikely), but something I've internalized from my collective experiences.

A writing professor will tell me one day that a writer needs discomfort to inspire him, a statement I'll generally find to be true. I have a strange relationship with the Debbie Downer inside of me. There is a small, dirty part of all of us that is never happier than when we needlessly feel down. I am intensely aware of oscillating back and forth between feeling absolutely fine with my state of being and feeding the flame in me, attached to that voice that tells me I can always be better, that someday soon I better figure out how to negotiate conversations or no one except my sister will want to be friends with me. Years in the future, I will still wonder at the elusive set of cues given off by facial expressions, body posture, and things left unsaid that lets other people communicate without constant clarification.

"You can't be perfect," my girlfriends, my mom, therapists, social workers, teachers, and aides will be fond of telling me.

"I know," I lie, casting my eyes down slightly.

Outside of the music room in elementary school, there will hang a poster depicting a spread of stars and a full moon situated against the backdrop of the night sky.

"Shoot for the moon. If you miss, you'll still land among the stars."

No, I think I'd swim from there. The light isn't far out of reach.

CHAPTER 3

ASPERGER'S

I can't decide if it's the poet or the Aspie in me that has it in for labels. It's a strange, telling phenomenon for a writer to loathe words, even briefly. But I can trace this contempt back to a moment I had in seventh grade, staring into my dad's kitchen while he washed dishes. I had just taken out the trash, and was trying to reel in my anxiety as I realized I wouldn't be back home at Mom's at the right time. I think everyone has moments in which the brain switches gears and for whatever reason finds itself firing on all cylinders.

My eyes fall on the cabinets, wooden, finished, and painted white. Cabinet. The word just seemed wrong to me, and I had to figure out why. I pulled out a notebook.

Calling the structures across the room by name assumed too much, I realized. Yes, they are cabinets. They hold my dad's snowman dishes (which we eat from even in July in defiance of the norm and because they're the biggest plates we have), but that doesn't do it justice. The whole history of the object is lost in what it is. We use the word "cabinet" because it isn't practical to remember that what sits in an apartment in New York was once at least one tree. Because of the shortcut the word provides, we don't have to think about how it was cut down, processed, and put together.

Even though labels are a crucial part of the best (only) system of communication we have, I still resent them because they can't tell the whole story.

You can imagine the mixed bag of feelings I carry about the Asperger's label. I have been both angry and grateful that "Asperger's syndrome" is only a phrase.

It's not a term with which I identify strongly. Perhaps, as I've been reminded by my cleverer friends, it's because "Asperger's" sounds uncannily like "ass burgers." It's just a name; I'd like to think it doesn't define me. The word is an opportunity to connect with others of the same distinction, and it's also a potential wedge threatening to widen the gap between my world and the shared world inhabited by others. Nevertheless, it ropes me in, makes me a part of its history and lineage.

As with any label, the label "Asperger's" comes with its own set of assumptions. For instance, several people have asked me:

"What are you good at? Do you have a special talent?"

They're thinking of *Rain Man* or something. For some reason, I want to be offended, but I have to admit that they're not wrong.

"Languages, English and others," I sometimes say. Even though some don't say it, I can see that they're surprised I didn't enthusiastically say "Chemistry" or "Math!"

But the inadequacy of labels is a poor reason to remain ill informed. So is laziness. So I cracked a book about my condition.

It's strange yet insightful to read research characterizing my disorder, by the man whose name I carry as a part of my own identity.

AUTISM VS ASPERGER'S

The children I will present all have in common a fundamental disturbance which manifests itself in their physical appearance, expressive functions, and, indeed, their whole behavior. This disturbance results in severe and characteristic difficulties of social integration. In many cases the social problems are so profound that they overshadow everything else. In some cases, however, the problems are compensated by a high level of original thought and experience. This can often lead to exceptional achievements in later life.[1]

---

1   Asperger, H. (1991 [1944]) "'Autistic Psychopathy' in Childhood" (trans. and annot. U. Frith) in Frith, U. (ed.) *Autism and Asperger Syndrome*. Cambridge: Cambridge University Press, p.37.

Autism was first used by Eugen Blueler to describe how schizophrenic patients withdrew from the world around them. It wasn't until the early 1940s that the term "autism" referred to its own specific disorder. Asperger explains that the term "autism" is derived from Blueler, but is used to describe individuals with a specific disorder. "While the schizophrenic patient seems to show progressive loss of contact, the children we are discussing lack contact from the start."[2]

The term "autism" came into being as describing its own disorder when Dr. Leo Kanner published his study in 1943, a year before Hans Asperger would publish his own paper. Separated by the Atlantic Ocean and World War II, Asperger didn't have access to Kanner's studies. Nevertheless, as Uta Frith states in *Autism and Asperger Syndrome*, the two agreed on the main features of autism, namely "The poverty of social interaction and the failure of communication; highlighted stereotypic behavior, isolated special interests, outstanding skills and resistance to change."[3]

One main difference in their respective publications is that Kanner's subjects had greater difficulty acquiring and using language than Asperger's did. Kanner's work is often said to describe those with early infantile autism, while Asperger's described children who lacked social ability but had a desire to fit in, who are "articulate yet ineloquent…gauche yet impractical, who are specialists in unusual fields."[4]

FACES AND NOISES

I am walking down the hall with Mrs. M, my speech therapist. It is towards the end of the day and I am heading back to class. The hallway is long with a red carpet. I know it is many hundreds of feet long; we measured the hundred feet from Mrs. G's classroom

---

2   Asperger, H. (1991 [1944]) "'Autistic Psychopathy' in Childhood" (trans. and annot. U. Frith) in Frith, U. (ed.) *Autism and Asperger Syndrome.* Cambridge: Cambridge University Press, p.39.

3   Frith, U. (1991) "Asperger and his Syndrome" in Frith, U. (ed.) *Autism and Asperger Syndrome.* Cambridge: Cambridge University Press, pp.10–12.

4   (Frith, pp.11–12)

door down past the water fountain once, so that we could see how long a blue whale was. I stare into the red of the carpet, trying to think about how a whale sounds. A book I used to read, *How Animals Communicate,* should have told me, but I can't remember. I start to move my mouth around, trying to hear the sound in my head as I attempt to make it.

Two sets of shoes invade my line of vision. I looked up to see Eric walking by with his helper. Everyone is always yelling at Eric to calm down, quiet down, and stop talking. He makes noises like I do, but he gets into a lot of trouble because he doesn't stop acting the way he does.

"Weep! Cubaweep," he shouts when he sees me. I am still trying to figure out how to make my best whale call. His aide hurries him past us and we both snicker. Even though she usually knows the answer, Laura will ask me for years who it is I'm talking to in the bathroom. For a long time, I'll wonder why "Making noises and faces makes me feel more comfortable" isn't an acceptable answer.

All of a sudden Mrs. M's hand is on me. She stops me and turns so that she is facing me. A shudder hard and cold goes through me when I realize that not only is Mrs. M not impressed with how realistic my whale call is, but also she is not happy. She brings her finger to the bridge of her nose and says to "look at me." I hate it when she does that. I shouldn't have to look; we can both hear each other just fine. I haven't realized yet it's also because I don't like to be reminded. But I look.

"Don't encourage him." Maybe it's the intensity of the situation, or the fact that I know Mrs. M will never understand. But I can't stop smiling.

"You think it's funny, don't you? It isn't funny and it's not cute. You think other people think it's funny when you do that?"

I don't have a real answer but my first reflex is to say "No," because her tone of voice tells me I should.

"Well it isn't. One of these days I'm going to bring in a camcorder, walk around and tape you if that's what it takes to show you what you sound like. Do you want that?"

"No!"

"Then you've got to *stop making noises!*"

My hairs stand up and my stomach clenches. A wave of what I will later know to be anxiety passes over me. I always feel like this when adults yell at me: scared and out in the open, my ears getting hot. Does Eric feel like this when his aide yells at him?

I will not be like Eric.

MAKING CORRECTIONS

The monitors glow blue, their cursors flickering. We are in the computer lab, typing things up. We have just finished writing lists of words we know. I know a lot of words and I like finding new ones. One time when I was getting out of swim lessons, I was trying to find all of the words that rhyme with duck, and my parents got mad when I used the "f" sound.

The printer makes too much noise and the edges of the pages are going to be hard to pull apart without ripping. My aide, Mrs. F, helps me with them.

"Fold them over once like this. Then fold them over again the opposite way."

She is hanging the paper just over the edge of the desk. She starts to tear and I look over to the other screens. Julie is announcing the letters as she types them.

"Pizza. P-I-T-S-A."

That isn't right. I start to move towards her.

"Dylan, now you try with the other side," Mrs. F asks.

I take the paper and fold it the way she showed me, but she has to remind me to watch what I'm doing. I get about halfway through and the paper rips a little. I frown and am about to throw the paper down but Mrs. F catches my arm.

"No, no. You just start from the other side," she says and then tears the paper. It is a letter I wrote to TJ because I was bored. My fingers usually can't find the keys fast enough to write down all that I'm thinking, but I get the letter done anyway. TJ is moving to California soon to live with his aunt. I hope he likes the letter. It says to have fun and I have an aunt in California too. I bet he'll be excited to know that.

Mrs. J, the computer lab lady, walks by me.

"Mrs. J, Julie spelled 'pizza' wrong!"

She stops, but she doesn't look as surprised as I thought she should. Not as much as I was.

"Why don't you go show her how to spell it?"

I walk over to Julie as fast as I can.

"Julie, that's not how you spell 'pizza.'"

"Yes it is." She is wearing a purple shirt and purple headband. It is not my favorite color. Green is.

"No, it's spelled 'P-I-Z-Z-A.' I know that doesn't sound right, but I asked my mom and dad about it. I don't know why the two Zs together make that sound, but they do."

Julie changes the letters on the screen. It's better.

I turn back to Mrs. F who shows me that TJ is leaving the room. I go to catch up with him and Mrs. J tells me to walk not run. TJ is a lot shorter than I am. People often think I'm older because I'm tall. I was disappointed when someone at therapy only thought I was eight, a year older. Sometimes they say nine or ten.

"You're moving to California. I have an aunt that lives there, she's nice. She came to visit three weeks ago."

I hand TJ the letter, but he's looking at me funny. His hat has a button right on the top of it. I feel the piece of paper come out of my hand, and my finger feels the rip I made earlier.

"Thanks."

But he doesn't say anything else. He just walks down the hall. The carpet in this hall is different. It is red, but it doesn't take up the whole floor. There are white linoleum tiles like the ones in my kitchen at home. Linoleum is a word I learned this year. I should have written that—

"Dylan, you have to use your indoor voice!" Mrs. F looks angry so I look away. But it's hard because she's close by. Some of the boys and girls in my class are looking at me, and so is the computer lady.

"And you were standing too close to TJ. You can't do that; you'll make people feel uncomfortable!"

Mrs. F is getting louder and I'm afraid more people are going to look. Like they look at Eric.

My hands are moving all by themselves now. It just feels right to move when I feel like this. Mrs. F is taking me out of the computer room.

Later that night, I find out that my aunt actually lives in North *Carolina.* I got it wrong, like Julie got "pizza" wrong. TJ will never know about the mistake, and for me that still doesn't seem right.

ACCORDING TO ASPERGER HIMSELF

Aspies are a group of individuals. I have yet to meet two that have the same quirks or areas of interest. However, I can't help but see myself in some of the descriptions Asperger gives, such as with Fritz V who exhibits characteristics of my preschool self.

> Posture, eye gaze, voice and speech made it obvious at first glance that the boy's relations to the outside world were extremely limited…he remained an outsider and never took much notice of the world around him. It was impossible to get him to join in group play, but neither could he play properly with himself. He just did not know what to do with the toys he was given…he put building blocks in his mouth…or threw them under the beds. The noise this created seemed to give him pleasure.[5]

Though I wasn't fond of mouthing objects, I certainly lived in a world of sound. Mrs. M and my other therapist constantly drew my attention to my echolalia; under my breath, I repeated the ends of my sentences and others'. Imitating speech and worldly sounds was one early method of connecting my world with the world around me.

Being among the first to notice autism, it would be unreasonable to imagine that Asperger was correct in all of his conclusions. However, I do find a kernel of myself even in some

---

5   Asperger, H. (1991 [1944]) "'Autistic Psychopathy' in Childhood" (trans. and annot. U. Frith) in Frith, U. (ed.) *Autism and Asperger Syndrome.* Cambridge: Cambridge University Press, p.42.

of the more controversial statements he made, even about "autistic acts of malice":

> With uncanny certainty, the children manage to do whatever is most unpleasant or hurtful in a given situation. However, since their emotionality is poorly developed, they cannot sense how much they hurt others, either physically, as in the case of younger siblings, or mentally, as in the case of parents.[6]

PLAY NICE

It's a cloudy day out. I follow Corey and a few other boys over to the side of the school where some of the kids race the buses as they come in, dropping more kids off. Corey and his friends are pushing each other, playing a game of cops and robbers. I saw something like this on TV once. This is where the good cop who pretends he's a bad guy takes the criminal and presses him for information.

I take Corey by the front of his leather jacket with all of my strength and push him up against the wall. He moves a lot easier than I thought he would and when he hits the wall his eyes look a lot bigger than normal.

I look away into the window we are near, and I see my speech therapist, Mrs. M, sitting at her desk and eating. It's weird to see teachers eating; they have lunch but no recess. I shake Corey a little bit, and I realize Mrs. M is standing up.

I know this moment. This is how I felt in the instant I pushed my sister while we were jumping on the bed. She was flying through the air and I realized there was nothing I could do about it. I threw my hands up and screamed in anticipation of Laura's crying, Mom's yelling. Mrs. M is moving her finger back and forth at me. She's coming to the window.

We run. I don't want to get into trouble. I can't get into trouble. My friend Cam and I run up the stairs to the jungle gym

---

6   Wing, L. (1991) "The relationship between Asperger's Syndrome and Kanner's autism" in Frith, U. (ed.) *Autism and Asperger Syndrome*. Cambridge: Cambridge University Press, p.77.

and across the swinging bridge. Just before the curving metal slide, we duck. The boards are very close together here, and I don't think Mrs. M can see us.

"Can she see us?" I ask Cam.

"I don't know."

I don't like hiding. I peer through a crack to see Mrs. M and a recess monitor walking around and looking. They are below us. I can't believe she doesn't see us.

"Should we go down?" Cam asks.

"No!" I whisper. Strange using my indoor voice outside.

But I look again and they're still standing down there, looking up. I can't just sit here like this. So I slide down.

"There you are!" Mrs. M comes shouting towards me. Her hair is short like Mom's but she's taller and scarier.

"Why were you doing that to Corey? That's not nice."

"We were just… I was playing…" The sun is coming out and pointing down right on me.

"Well it didn't look like you were playing. It looked like you were hurting him!"

I try to tell her, but my words come out wrong, too fast, and in chunks. I am getting into trouble. My ears get warmer and I have to squint because of the sun.

Later, at home, when my eyes and nose stop running, Mom sits with me, explaining.

"Dylan, I'm not mad anymore. You're not going to get into trouble. You apologized to Corey, right?"

"Yes I did."

"Okay. Maybe you shouldn't play detective for a little—"

"Cops and robbers."

"Dylan, you're interrupting."

"Sorry."

Sometimes I remember to wait my turn, and sometimes I don't. Sometimes what I have to say feels too important, like when I need to correct them. I'll still interrupt even through college, raising my hand and considering what I have to say next rather than listening to what someone else is saying. I will wonder if I have actually improved or changed slightly. Maybe I will have just learned how to hide better.

"Maybe you should find other games to play besides cops and robbers. I know you didn't mean to scare Corey and you didn't want to hurt him. But Mrs. M didn't know that. She claims it looked like you were mad at him."

"I wasn't. I told her that. Corey wasn't even hurt."

"I know. Dylan, you're bigger than the other kids. It would be very easy for you to hurt them accidentally."

I tell her "okay" and look down. This reminds me of the time I saw the obese man in the hospital and announced in front of my occupational therapist Eileen that he was fat. As for now, Mom doesn't seem to be too upset, and since I didn't hurt anyone, I won't get into trouble at school.

"REFRIGERATOR MOTHERS"—
THE TROUBLE WITH
VILLAINIZING PARENTS

Dr. Bruno Bettelheim was the one to coin the term "refrigerator mother" from Freudian theory. The basic assumption was that the autism and the misbehavior that went along with it were the results of bad parenting. Kanner himself disregarded the theory, as did others such as Richard Pollack with his book *The Creation of Dr. B.*

Though the theory was popular through the 1970s, and has largely been debunked, it is unreasonable to think that parents of autistic children don't feel blame. The truth is they feel blame even when they shouldn't have to, especially when faced with criticism.

My mother and I were walking through the grocery store (I must have been around four or five) and we came to the broccoli. I was convinced that I liked broccoli because it was my favorite color: green. But what I repeatedly failed to remember was that the texture of the broccoli horrified me; I would often spit it right out. This day, my mother was adamant. No, I couldn't have any broccoli. I stomped and begged, yet she kept saying "no." Just as she told me that I could instead have one of the free cookies the store offered, an elderly woman walked by. Not having understood the particulars of the situation, this woman gave my mother hell for denying me healthy food.

"How dare you!?" I imagine this woman screaming at my mother, who was trying to push her distraught son along and get through this store sometime today. People probably started to watch as the old woman backed down, ending her mini-tirade. Mom would have shaken it off, paying attention to the task at hand.

There's a difference between "I won't" and "I can't." The misconception is that people with disabilities like mine are simply being difficult when we don't follow directions exactly. A teacher might ridicule me for not paying attention in class or for speaking out of turn or disrupting. The parents of higher-functioning autistic kids are often the subjects of ridicule when a report such as this one comes back to them.

"If only you would discipline him, not give in to him, etc., he'd be better behaved."

Because some of us function well enough to pass or even excel academically, teachers, professionals, and other students have a tendency to be less understanding of social difficulty. But the fact is that maybe at the time I was incapable of paying attention rather than being unwilling to. The light in the classroom may have been too bright at the time; we might have had a shift in routine (group work instead of scheduled math class); there may simply have been a beehive of voices talking at once that left me incapable of focusing my attention on any given thing. I would not have understood why dinosaur noises and out-of-context cartoon quotes would be disruptive to class.

Certainly, not all of my behavior was a result of the autism. Sometimes I was just being a stinker, like the time my sister and I wouldn't stay quiet in church, or a meltdown I had in the middle of Toys "R" Us because I was being denied a Matchbox car. Much of the time, it's more complicated than either. I *can't* put the buttons on my shirt or pants through the holes, but I *won't* put a jacket on in thirty degree weather. I think I picked up on this complication early and used it to my advantage. I noticed that with every anxious apology, my mom's tirade over me not having remembered to put her important outfit into the dryer on time faded into sympathy for me. I'll never admit how long I used this defense mechanism.

Some of the teachers and professionals at my first elementary school openly disliked my mother and undoubtedly thought that my behavior was a result of poor parenting on her part. Now, I understand that it can be a complicated issue. For instance, when I was about three, Mom had me psychologically evaluated. This story is a favorite of hers early on during workshops.

"Dylan went into the room to be tested and there was a one-way mirror, so I was able to watch as he was being tested. I didn't know what to expect, but I had some confidence; I knew Dylan was a smart kid. But when the evaluator started to show Dylan colors, numbers, shapes, and letters, he wouldn't respond. And these were all things that Dylan was already familiar with. So when Dylan was done and we were walking down the hall, I asked him, confused and quite frankly a little upset, what had happened.

'Dylan, you know your shapes and your letters, why didn't you tell the man when he asked?'

Dylan looked at me and told me flat out: 'Mommy that man didn't know his shapes or his colors or anything, and I wasn't going to tell him!'"

In first and second grade, I apparently did not appear visibly disabled enough to receive swift and adequate accommodations. This reluctance to give me full accommodations is partially understandable in light of the fact that the time I was diagnosed happened to be about the time that Asperger's Syndrome was becoming its own separate diagnosis. Dr. Asperger's article wasn't available and translated into English until the early 1990s. Therefore, the teachers and special education professionals at that school district were largely unfamiliar with the disorder. But to some extent, ignorance of the law really is no excuse.

Among those familiar with autism was an early teacher of mine. I later found out that she has a son with autism much more severe than mine. She was often happy to insinuate that not only did I not have autism but also the bad behaviors I did have were almost surely the result of bad parenting. One professional even told my mother explicitly: "This child is a floodgate. If I give him accommodations, I have to give everyone else accommodations." It is our theory that some of the nastiness teachers and therapists showed me throughout my stay in the district was a direct result of how much they really disliked my mother. They didn't want to appear as if they weren't in the know; and it was probably much easier to see my mom as unreasonable and militant.

THE REASON I INTERRUPT

"Did you know that the male Siberian tiger can be up to—"

Mrs. F takes a white card out of her stack and slides it across the table to me. "Interrupting" the card says. It has a picture of two faces looking at each other with their mouths open and another face off to the side with its mouth open wide. Brittany and Evan look back at me and Mrs. G stops talking, looks at me, then keeps on talking about other animals. I don't want this card, so I push it back at Mrs. F.

"You don't need to tell me—"

Mrs. F pushes the "interrupting" card back towards me and takes out another card. This one says "indoor voice."

"But I *was* using my indoor voice!"

There is less noise all of a sudden. The rest of the boys and girls are starting to look over here—stupid Mrs. F and her cards. We were talking about other animals, and I bet the class doesn't know how big tigers can get. Everyone's looking now, and I'm not happy.

"Alright, come on. That was it. Come with me, we're going to go see Mrs. M."

"No!"

"Dylan, go with Mrs. F!" Mrs. G says. Mrs. F and I are the only ones moving, and I can feel all their eyes. The hallway is long (at least two-and-a-half blue whales), even longer when everyone's mad at me.

After the adults whisper to each other for a while, I sit down at a table, and Mrs. M is across from me with Mrs. F next to me.

"I understand you're giving Mrs. F quite a hard time. I thought we'd talked about this. Your mother even came in and we talked for a *long* time about this. So what's going on?"

I want to grunt and scream and sigh. I feel bad for Mrs. F now, but they just don't understand. I shrug.

"Well, we're going to have to figure something out, because you can't be coming down here every time something goes wrong in class."

I could start to say a lot of different sentences right now, but I want to say them all.

"I was just, ahhh. I wanted…hrrm…it's annoying, agh."

"What's annoying?"

"It's the cards. Everyone looks when Mrs. F gives me a card, it makes me feel bad."

"Dylan, that's *why* she gives you the cards. Your mom said you were getting embarrassed when Mrs. F tells you out loud to use your indoor voice or be quiet. I bet you wouldn't give your mother a hard time like this. So why are you doing it to Mrs. F, huh?"

I don't know what to say. Even my own mom has embarrassed me like this. This year, she's my teacher for religious education. Once, when Brittany came into the room and I fell over in my chair really flat as a board, like the skunk that's in love with the cat on the cartoons, some of the other kids started to talk when it wasn't their turn, and then my mom said something.

"Dylan has something called autism, and that's why he sometimes says the things he says or behaves a certain way. But he can't help it." Everyone behaved better after that. Even me. But I remember wondering almost angrily whether or not she had the right to put me on the spot like that. What if I didn't want people to know that I had Asperger's, even if that does help the situation? Let them figure it out for themselves if they can. Mike walked up to me after class and told me that he felt sorry for me.

"Why? I don't feel sorry." I won't realize this is at least half a lie until I develop the mental faculties and years of experience for meaningful introspection. I do know that even though my whole class now knows I have autism (thanks, Mom) I'm sort of glad Mike felt sorry for me.

And I don't think Mrs. M feels that way at all.

"I'll be quiet."

"Will you? Good. 'Cause if you're not, we'll have to have another talk with your mom about whether or not we should just forget about these cards. Now will you apologize to Mrs. F?"

UNWELCOME NEWS

I don't know what's wrong, but Mommy doesn't look right. She is waiting for me in front of the house and tells me "hi" when I come off of the bus. When I get into the house and we take off my shoes and coat, she tells me to come into the family room with her. I still don't understand why we can't sit in the regular living room with the nice couches and piano, but for some reason we never do. In the family room, the T.V. is off and that makes it feel more serious.

The worst thing for me about a big change, I'll realize later, is when I don't see it coming up on the horizon. Change is the enemy for one dependent on the status quo, and an unseen enemy is that much more vicious.

"Come sit down, Punky D." She's always called me that, and she told me it has something to do with how my hair used to stick up when I was younger. It won't start to embarrass me for years yet, when I'll be convinced that she does it to embarrass me slightly. I sit on the couch next to her and she reaches over to the table. There are two new books, and one of them has turtles on the cover. I am excited for a second at the thought of two new books until I recognize a word on the cover.

Divorce.

"Dylan, your father and I are separating. I went out and got a couple of books I think will help you understand."

My eyes are watering and there are so many things I want to say. My mind is trying to realize that an era is ending. Gone will be the times like when Mom and Dad called each other "hon" and taught us together how to ride bikes, or wrote each other notes in front of Laura and me to hide whatever it was they were saying about each other. I would have been comforted if there were any way to know that by middle and high school it will be almost unbearable for Laura and me to experience the awkwardness of my parents sitting in a room together for more than a few minutes.

Before I can say anything, she opens the book with the turtles on it. The emotion I'm feeling now will turn into one of the major frustrations I'll have with my mother. She has an organizational quality about her which she uses to make any car into a conference room. Any time is a perfect time to get our agenda in order. Any time is a great time to look about four or five steps into the future.

In the book are a turtle mom, a turtle dad, and two turtle kids. The turtles' faces turn down in frowns when they find out that their parents are getting a divorce. It's making my eyes water more. "What did we do wrong?" one of the turtle kids asks.

"Why are you and Daddy splitting?" I ask before mom can go on reading. She sighs and turns the book so that it's facing open into her lap.

"Now I'm going to tell you the same thing I'm going to tell Laura. Your dad and I haven't been getting along like we used to. We've been arguing—not about you and Laura—but we've been arguing. This sometimes happens to parents. But just because we aren't together doesn't mean we don't love you. Your dad and I disagree on some things, but we both want you to know that it isn't your fault and it isn't Laura's fault. Do you understand that?"

I am really crying now, and that makes it twice as hard to talk. I didn't need a book about turtles to tell me that it isn't my fault Mom and Dad are separating, that they both still love me. I've done nothing wrong, nothing that bad.

"I don't…are we…moving? Or is Dad moving? I like this house!"

"We're not moving, hon. Dad is going to be moving out, but he is staying just until he finds a place to live."

I remember feeling exactly this way when I realized I was moving into first grade. No longer would I have at least half of a day to spend at home with Mom and Laura. School would take all day now.

Laura and I are sitting at dinner with Mom and Dad. No one is talking, and I'm pushing my potatoes around on my plate with a fork. Usually, Mom tells me not to use all of my fingers to hold it, but today she's not saying anything. Neither is Dad. That's really strange. He's not eating much either. Laura is quiet, but she's eating. She holds the fork the right way. Mom must have cleaned the kitchen, because the counters look really, really white. The coffee maker and coffee grinder are sitting next to each other by the sink. Mommy hardly ever uses them, but Daddy uses them every day. Lots of loud noises bother me, but the coffee maker isn't one of them; I like it. The kitchen isn't going to look or sound right without it. What will I do?

I look over to Dad. His hair is messy and his moustache twitches while he takes a bite. He takes off his glasses and rubs his eyes. His face doesn't look right without the glasses. When is Daddy leaving? Where will he go? Mommy told me he's leaving soon and he won't be going far. But I need to know more than that.

My mind is away from the meal again, and I'm looking around. Our kitchen table and our dining room table have four chairs, one for each of us. I like our kitchen the way it is. I like our house the way it is. I'm crying again. I don't like the way crying feels. I don't like the way no one is saying anything. Why can't things stay the way they are so that I can get used to them?

"Daddy, I don't want you to leave, it's making me cry!"

"I don't want to leave either," Dad says in a voice that sounds too high and squeaky to be his. He gets up out of the chair.

"Let's stand up and cry together."

I stand up and hug him and we both cry loudly. Laura is tearing up. I look over at Mom, who sighs and puts down her fork.

Mom and Dad will make concerted efforts at not making the other parent sound like the bad guy. They will both be guilty of asking Laura and me what the other says about them.

Dad appears not to have seen the divorce coming anymore than I did. I'm too young and imperceptive to see my father's depression or my mother's anxiety. Years later, Dad will tell me some of his side of the story:

"Your mother is the one who decided we can't be together. We would have been a lot better off financially." But his voice will carry a knowing tone of acceptance. The divorce, like my autism, isn't something anyone wants. But with my father depressed, my mother miserable, and both Laura and me in the balance, something has to give.

"I'm not going far—I'm never going to move far away. And just 'cause I don't live with you doesn't mean I'm not your father, okay? Remember that," he tell us before he leaves.

CHAPTER 4

THE MOVE

Since long before my diagnosis, Mom devoted herself to the way of life of my routine and the cause of helping me move beyond my obstacles. Though I know she would say she had no choice in the matter, this decision was not an easy one to follow.

I have heard Mom say: "When one person in the family has autism, the whole family has autism." Everyone feels it. I went to therapy every afternoon during Laura's formative years, meaning that she didn't get a nap. She is still incapable of taking naps to this day, even when she's exhausted. My rigidity loosened its grip on our household only slowly. Times of transition often caused tantrum events that might hold the whole house hostage until I calmed down.

But change happened anyway. Often the changes that I feared most were the ones that turned out for the best. Though seven-year-old Dylan didn't understand at the time, and though the ripples from that event still touch and complicate our lives, the divorce would prove to make our lives easier.

We got two dogs, Sarah and Cocoa, within the space of a year. Our collie–retriever mix Sarah came on Valentine's Day, and I cried and cried because my young mind was set on getting a teacup poodle. But I got over this unexpected kink in my plan early. Getting two dogs wasn't a tough decision. I suppose Laura and I would have been receiving allergy shots long enough by then to have overcome whatever allergies we had to long-haired dogs. But the dogs did end up complicating our family life. I remember, when Dad came over to pick us up, how strange it felt to know that this dog would never be his. He took an instant liking to Sarah and then to our black Lab–springer spaniel mix. Mom attempted to set up clear boundaries with Dad from the start, but this became difficult when she needed someone to let the dogs out while we were gone. Dad came in every chance he could to say hello to the dogs, and despite a couple of phases Mom went through over the years when she let Dad into the house as little as possible, she eventually gave in.

Moving in the middle of the school year to a house in Binghamton, with two kids (one autistic, the other artistic), two dogs (one calm but food oriented, one crazy but also insanely loyal), and a career change on the horizon, must have meant quite a slew of tough decisions in itself.

The divorce meant that the hill home with the walk-in closets and extra living room was definitely unaffordable. Laura and I would both have to switch schools. But Mom had the necessary improvements made to the paint job, the tiling, and the landscaping. The tiny pond and odd shed in the back had to go. With the help of family friends we moved all of our stuff. Laura happened to choose the bigger room, which infuriated me because I was used to having the biggest room. My new room was little more than half the size of my old one, painted blue instead of the black I had asked for. The dogs had to be walked out the back door to the kennel area and often slipped out of the grasp of our young fingers.

The move also meant that I would be changing school districts. Of course, that had been my mother's intention after having to go in to the school and defend my right to special accommodations. Despite the breakdowns and anxieties that would no doubt accompany switching elementary schools and houses, Mom hoped the move would mark a welcome change in my schooling environment.

The transition in schools is a story my mom always comes back to during our presentations to illustrate a point.

"I went to enroll them both in the school closest to our home, which was a really nice school in a good neighborhood. I went in and spoke with the principal. I told him 'My daughter is in first grade. She's smart, she's well behaved, and you'll love her. My son is in second grade, he's smart, he's well behaved…he also has Asperger's Syndrome. But you'll love him, too.' He looked at me and said, I kid you not:

'Oh, I don't take those here. I only have eight left and if he goes here, he'll be in the one classroom with severely disabled kids and you really don't want that for him.'

I was speechless. My jaw dropped and I just looked at him. He said:

'I'll deny all of this conversation. It's only me and you in this room. Why don't you take him to the school up the road, I hear the principal at that school takes a lot of those.'

So I went home. And I cried. Because I hadn't expected this type of reaction from this new district. I could have challenged him, and I would have; he was in the wrong. But at that point I was so tired of fighting, and would it really have been worth it?

So, I decided to give the school up the road a try. Now this school was vastly different from the neighborhood school. There was a lot more economic diversity and hardship, and the majority of students qualified for free or reduced lunch. But the reception we got could not have been more different from the other school we'd been to…"

A NEW CLASS, A NEW START

Everything here is so much different. This new school is a lot bigger than my old one and I can't tell if the playground is better or not. When Mom and I step through the front doors there's a huge picture of a superhero with an eagle's head. The eagles. I guess I am going to be an eagle now. I remember when I was younger I made a poem about eagles' claws. I wished my hands were eagles' claws, because then they could be my friends. Why couldn't it have been a tiger on the wall?

A woman comes up to Mom and me and talks to Mom for a minute. I hear the name "Vallentino." My new school, this is hard to believe. I'm not going to see any of my older classmates here, and that seems very strange. A man in a suit comes out of the door that says "Main Office." A woman calls him "Mr. Brown." We move away from him down the hallway. The floors here are white like the kitchen (linoleum?), and no red rugs, just mats near the doors. These are big hallways, who knows how many (blue whales) hundreds of feet long. We pass classrooms that have their art projects posted on the walls.

We turn another corner. And some of the tiles are green. Drawings of vegetables and milk and posters on the wall with cows, basketball players, and food pyramids make me think we're walking past a door to the cafeteria. I'm glad we found that. I've got to remember where this is, because I'm already starting to feel hungry.

The woman leading us stops at a door that says "Mrs. Valentino." Mom and I walk into the classroom. Mrs. Valentino stands up from behind her desk. She is shorter and thinner than my old teacher. She looks like she's nicer, too.

Mrs. Valentino says hello to Mom and then introduces herself to me.

"Class, we have a new student. Everyone say hello to Dylan!"

"Hi, Dylan." It always sounded funny to me when a teacher makes the whole class say the same thing at the same time. Everyone had nametags on his or her desk. "Brittany" reads the one in front of the girl who had been whining loudly to another boy before the teacher had stopped the class. Which of these will turn out to be my friends?

While Mom talks to Mrs. Valentino, I walk down a row of desks. I walk up to two Asian boys. Maybe they are Japanese, then I could use some of the phrases I learned with them.

"I speak Japanese," I tell them, waiting for a response.

"We're not Japanese," one of them tells me.

"We're Vietnamese," the other finishes.

Their name tags read "Ron" and "Tran."

"I know," I lied. "This is how you introduce yourself: Watashi no numaewa Dylan dez."

Tran and Ron don't say anything. They're just looking at me. I hear my mom talking to Mrs. Valentino. The boys and girls (my new classmates, still hard to believe) are talking to each other.

"Where did you move from?" Ron asks.

"Johnson City," I say, looking out the window. I can see a little bit of the lower level of the new playground. The sky is too bright and I can't look long. I watch the bright spots cover the walls and disappear.

"My room is smaller than the one at my other house. But there's a laundry chute and it was built before nineteen twenty. "

"Oh."

MAKING FRIENDS

No matter how many times I have rehearsed and thought of answers to the question of when it was I finally developed the ability to make friends, my words get caught in the circuitry on the way out of my mouth. It isn't an easy question to answer, especially if it's asked by a girl I am trying to impress at the time or by a parent sitting next to a possible Aspie, usually tucked into a video game or a book, or staring slightly into space.

The first time I got asked this question in front of a group of people (people I was being paid to give relevant and interesting information to) I stumbled through an uncertain answer.

"Well, it's...a little bit hard to say. I know that the more I broke down the walls of what I call 'my own world', the more I became socially integrated into this one. And that quite frankly took a lot of time, effort, and awkward social interactions. I would say sometime during elementary school..." I looked at Mom for guidance while I fumbled.

"It might have even been early middle school, Dylan." She paused, facing the audience. I don't want to disagree with her in front of a group of people; I have a bit more respect than that. But my mom has a certain tendency to exaggerate. As they say, memory is reconstructive (damn it).

"For a long time, certainly through preschool and early elementary, Laura was really Dylan's playmate. They would disappear for hours at a time playing Batman or other very intricate role-playing games with specific sets of rules. But a few years after Dylan went to school and started to be exposed to that world of social interaction he began to try to make friends other than Laura."

I took it from there. "I never had quite as many friends as I wanted. The more I realized that there was another world of social hierarchy, the more I wanted to be at the top of it. I wanted to be one of the real popular kids who everyone said hi to. I wanted to have more friends than anyone."

At one of the last presentations we gave, the parent who asked this question had a little girl with slightly frizzy hair and glasses sitting next to her. I was just getting to the part where I explained my desire for friends (which would grow to be nearly obsessive by high school), when I caught sight of this little girl. She had interrupted the presentation earlier to make sure we knew that the Batman costume six-year-old Dylan was wearing in one of the PowerPoint slides was the wrong color. I remember thinking that I would have been extremely curious to see where this girl was at in a few years.

Optimism is essential, but it must be coupled with fierce realism. Whether she realizes it or not, this is a lesson Mom has taught me.

"But it didn't exactly happen that I became the most popular kid overnight, no matter how much I'd like to stand up here and tell you that story tonight. As early as I can remember having friends, I've always had a few very good friends. As much as I wanted to blend in with the rest of my classmates, I have always been drawn to those most like myself. At first this meant that I hung out with other autistic kids. But even as I did make friends with non-learning-disabled kids, they have always tended to be more open-minded, dare I say 'weird,' ones. Even having one friend who 'got' me did wonders. And at first, that person was my sister."

DADDY WEEKENDS

Sometimes when I read, people think I'm not paying attention. I know I am in a car on my way somewhere when I read in a car. I can hear the music when I read in front of a radio or a television. So when the side door opens downstairs, I know Laura is home. But even though the sound is loud and Mom will ask me to come downstairs soon, I can't stop reading. Right now, I'm reading a *Goosebumps* book about a teacher that's really a monster in disguise. Every time I get to the end of a chapter, it seems like it's just getting to the good part. I really wonder how RL Stine does that.

I keep reading even though Sarah and Cocoa are barking and running around downstairs. It doesn't stop me from seeing and hearing in my mind what is going on in the book. Dad tells me that I shouldn't read the way I do, but I didn't know that I mouth the words that I read when I read them. I'm still doing it now.

"Dylan! Laura's home!"

"Dylan!" Laura screams.

"Hi!"

There are only a couple more pages left until the end of the chapter and I know something is going to happen. It won't take long. Sarah is still barking and I can hear Cocoa's claws against the ceramic tile and Mom yelling at her, "Cocoa! No jumping!" She's part springer spaniel and part black Lab. That means she would be a good hunting dog, she likes water, and she likes to jump.

"Dylan, come on down and get a snack, I have to leave soon!"

"I'm almost done! One more page and it will be the end of the chapter!"

I know Mom has to go to class again tonight in Elmira. I'm almost done with this page and then there's only a little bit of a page left. Downstairs, Mom is opening drawers and cabinets. I am getting hungry, but something is about to happen, I know it.

Now there's someone on the stairs. It's Laura, and one of the dogs is coming up behind her. There's only a paragraph left.

There's a knock on the door and Laura comes in. She cut all of her hair off not too long ago so that she'd look more like one of her friends, but then she cried. It's growing back now, but for a long time I wished it would grow fast, because Laura didn't look right.

"Dylan, Mom says you have to come down. Not two minutes, now. 'Cause she has to leave soon and Dad is going to be here."

Laura speaks with the giddy, matter-of-fact tone I think all little sisters share when faced with the opportunity to tell their older brothers what to do.

Sarah, our collie–golden retriever mix runs into my room. She and Cocoa have already made poop stains on the light blue carpet. There are more in Laura's room than in mine, and it makes the floors look older. Did she really have to come in?

"Just one more—"

"Sarah, no!"

I put the Agent Scully bookmark I got from Mom back into the book and close it. Sarah has caught a tissue in her long muzzle and is going under my bed with it. Did she have to let Sarah in?

Sarah is squatting down to try to get under my bed. I jump off and try to catch her, but she's fast and the top half of her is already under, and I can't grab onto her overly-furry back side. What if she gets sick? I don't remember what's in the tissue or why the tissue was on the floor. I reach under after her, trying to get to her mouth.

"Sarah, NO! Get back here!" I scream. She's not supposed to be eating tissues, "No, no, no, no!"

I try to open her mouth, but she's done chewing and she's trying to swallow.

"No! Laura, she's going to choke, she's going to get sick, she's going to—"

"What is going *on* up there?"

Sarah is scooting out from under the bed. Her ears are back, and she runs past Laura and me before we can grab her. We follow her out of the room.

"What if she gets sick, what if she throws up, what if—"

Sarah flies down the stairs. At the bottom, she runs past Mom through the entryway (called a foyer, I'm told) and into the kitchen.

"Sarah ate a tissue and now Dylan's freaking out," Laura says.

"Sarah," Mom calls after the dog. But she doesn't sound worried. She sounds the way people sound when they aren't happy but have already given up.

"Mom! Mom! What if she gets hurt, what if—"

"Dylan, it's okay, she's a dog. She'll be just fine."

"But—"

"DYLAN. You need to calm down. Trust me, she will be just fine. We've just got to start doing a better job keeping garbage in the garbage so that Sarah and Cocoa can't get it."

"Are you sure?"

"I'm sure. Take some breaths and go into the kitchen. I made you a peanut butter and jelly."

I trust Mom, but I'm mad at Sarah still. What if she grabs a tissue with something poisonous in it? What if she eats something else that would be bad for her?

Cocoa is curled up in the dog carrier in the dining room. Mom always says Cocoa doesn't like yelling and that's why she hides when things get crazy in the house. Laura says Cocoa is my dog because she's like me. We both make funny faces. We don't like loud noises. We have the same birthday. I feel bad now, so I pet her. She looks like she's frowning. Laura's right.

Our kitchen still looks new to me; our old one didn't have a center island, skylights, or an electric can opener. The fridge is new, too.

"Mommy, is this weekend a Mommy weekend?" Laura asks. It should be written right on the calendar that Mom puts on the freezer, but it's the beginning of the month and last month's calendar is up.

"It's a Daddy weekend," I say. Laura frowns. I think she likes Mommy weekends better. Daddy weekends mean we go with Daddy at four on Friday night and come back before four on Sunday.

I hear an engine turning off outside, and both Sarah and Cocoa run to the front door to start barking. It's a truck's engine. Dad is here. I look at the clock in the kitchen. Four oh five. Dad's late, but I know Mom doesn't really have to leave for another twenty minutes.

Laura has told me that she wishes Mom and Dad were still together, and I remember she used to ask Mom a lot if they would get back together, even after I knew they wouldn't. At first I wanted them to stay together, too. It still seems weird that Dad lives in an apartment by himself with a different phone number and a car that Mom doesn't ever drive.

But today is a Dad day, and we usually go to the mall. As the years go on and we get to the homework age, we will sit in Arby's and do it there until that drives Mom crazy. I will grow to miss strangers telling Laura how good the drawing of a dog looks.

The complications from the divorce won't work themselves out for quite some time. Dad will take us kayaking and leave us on the shore of a lake by ourselves for long enough for me to get nervous. Laura will tell me for a while with an authority in her voice she could only have learned from Mom (it's sort of like an older sister voice) to calm down already before she gets anxious herself. He will lose track of me in a store, and my anxiety will make me ask a store clerk to help me. More than once, he will take us to Buffalo to see our grandma for a weekend and call on Sunday at eight at night to tell my mom we'll be staying another day. We were supposed to be home at four, I'll remind him until he's ready to crack. There will be a period of about two weeks when Dad isn't allowed to see us because custody is still in question.

But Dad keeps his word—he never goes anywhere. What now just seems like the chaotic wash of life is really the beginnings of a new life rhythm and the birth of memories—weekends alternately spent hiking or biking or watching westerns with Dad, and taking the dogs to the park or getting the lawn done or ordering a pizza or going to Elmira to visit our other grandma with Mom.

THE NINJA TURTLES' LAST STAND

It's lunch time at Woodrow Wilson Elementary school. On the lower level, a bunch of fourth graders are playing football with Mr. G. They keep shouting "it's first down" or "it's second down." It goes up to four, but I don't know what a "down" is. I've played with them a couple of times but I don't really understand how the game works. I had to keep asking "Are we on offense or defense?" There are at least two games of tag happening in and around the jungle gym. Some first graders are trying to run up a slide.

Steven, Jared, and I have our own corner. On the blacktop between the woodchips and the corner where two fences come together, we play our own games. Today, we're playing *Teenage Mutant Ninja Turtles*. I pick the character I always pick—Casey Jones, the only good guy who isn't a mutant. I gave Casey a bunch of cool weapons like razor-blade hockey sticks and make him a master of martial arts like the turtles. Now Jared and Steven want to play as my character, so I have to be sure to choose first. I do let them use Casey on their birthdays. But I tell them they just have to make their characters cool like I did. Casey is my character.

Steven, Jared, and I are battling foot soldiers over near the fences, which we are pretending are electric. The foot soldiers fall down easily when we kick or punch them. I could make it so that they didn't, but the game's better when you're winning. Steven, playing Michelangelo, has to go back to Splinter to be healed when Beebop and Rocksteady shoot his shell with lasers.

"Why did you have to do that, Jared? Now I gotta choose another character and that's my favorite."

"'Cause that's the way it happens in the cartoon!"

"We're not going by the cartoon."

Before Jared can say anything, a boy I don't know comes up to us. He has a stick.

"When you're pretending to play a game with swords, you should get sticks and fight with those. It works better, 'cause then you don't forget who has what weapon."

Jared takes the stick over his head and swings it and it drops out of his hand and onto the ground.

"Just let us play the way we play," Steven tells the boy, who shrugs and walks away. He's wrong. We use more weapons other than swords. If I pick up a stick, I'm holding a stick. But if I pretend I'm holding a hockey stick, a baseball bat, or a different weapon, I can see it better in my head than if I had a stick.

"Pretend I'm...Donatello!" Steven shouts. He's short and a bit chubby, and he runs slowly because of the braces on his legs.

But I think Donatello is his best Turtle. Jared has been playing Leonardo. The way he's holding his pretend swords isn't right. But I don't say anything. Mom told me that he has trouble with his hands even more than I do. And he has autism, which makes him hum and wring his hands out like a cloth if he gets upset. I really wish he wouldn't do that during the game; it makes it harder for me to think about what happens next.

"What are you playing over there, Power Rangers?" some kid I don't know asks before he runs away with some of the other football kids.

Why do they always think we're playing Power Rangers? The boy is laughing and pointing at us, and his friends start to laugh.

The boys playing tag all run and jump off of the jungle gym away from the kid that is "it."

The lunch monitor starts to ring the cowbell that harbingers the end of recess, and we all have to go inside. The football boys are already in there, but for some reason I think I can still hear their laughing.

"Alright, until the next episode," Jared shouts, swinging his hands over his head like Mickey from Fantasia. Steven starts to try to run, but he staggers. A couple of girls behind him are watching.

Maybe tomorrow I'll play tag.

CHAPTER 5

THE BREAK

Even in the bright light of retrospect, it's nearly impossible to figure out how it is we became the people we became. The Buddhists say that even the self changes in such a way that it can only be considered fluid, never static (a terrifying thought to someone whose existence hinges almost entirely on an unchanging routine). We change our habits, our tastes, and our desires without warning, but seldom realize the depth and effect of these changes. This fact of invisible change has always unsettled me. I remember standing in the mirror, upset at the fact that I couldn't notice my growth day to day. That sort of change happens slowly, I was told. I never liked changes. I preferred to be informed of and in control of my reality. How can I be in control when I don't know how, when, or why things are changing, why *I* am changing? I have a bad habit of trying to master the currents rather than go with the flow.

If I have to change, I want to be the author of that change. Sometime during fourth grade, I decided I had heard one too many smart-ass Power Rangers comments at recess. What was it that clicked in me when I looked at my fellow Ninja Turtles one day and not only felt embarrassed for myself, but for them, too? Even when they weren't playing the games, they would give themselves away as disabled without ever knowing it. Their uneven gait, unnatural speech inflections, and anxious mannerisms made them painfully obvious. Association with them would mean others saw me as different too. This was possibly the first time I realized I wanted to be a bit more of a chameleon than that. Finally, I had heard a classmate snickering and realized that the snickering was directed *at me*. It wasn't cool to be running around pretending we knew Karate, kicking at enemies no one could see. At least, others didn't think so.

I know I didn't understand that change isn't instantaneous. As much as I would have liked to think otherwise, switching my Beach Boys CDs to *Now That's What I Call Music!* CDs didn't make me instantly cooler. But by starting to play tag, I was making one step (albeit a small one) up the ladder of cool. The tag kids played in snow or sleet, heat, or wind. It was their thing, and it became mine. Tag was a step in the right direction. It was fun, but it was something normal kids did. In my mind, I was abandoning my immature world of cartoon characters for real world fun.

In reality, I was substituting one fantasy world for another. Instead of kicking at the air and referencing superhero movies, we ran around referencing *Scooby-Doo* ("women and cowards first!"). In the same manner I used to convince my sister to play with toys the wrong way, according to rules I had only just thought of, the tag kids convinced me that the jungle gym was not to be used only as directed. We leaped from the tip-top of the towering wooden structures and ran up slides. We'd do anything short of killing ourselves not to be "it."

I FALL

The sun shines bright above the clouds today, and gusts of wind part our hair as we run. A minute ago, Mike tagged Steven, yelling "No tag-backs," and we all scattered. I have that complicated feeling you get when you know someone is following right behind you. It's fun because if I get caught it won't hurt, but it's terrifying because I know I might get caught. No one wants to be "it," mostly because it can take forever to tag someone else. Everyone runs away from you, acts like you're toxic. If you're "it" too long, you start to feel bad about yourself.

Steven is slower than I am, though, and I lose him by ducking under the jungle gym. I have hit my head on the piece of wood that makes up the top of the doorway more times than I can count, and I will one day jokingly attribute my hard head to such moments. The other players have scattered amongst the recess crowd. I am still the closest to Steven, and in my peripheral I can see everyone watching the chase.

He's closer behind than I thought; I'll have to lose him on the jungle gym. I bound up the stairs past a couple of second graders playing pirates and stop at the top. I could hook my arms under the purple bars in front of me and slide down, but it might take too long. There are too many kids clogging up the slide, so I can't escape left. And some dummy is standing in front of the fireman pole. Steven, quite a bit heftier than me, is chugging up the stairs.

When I first started playing tag, I felt odd running up the slide, letting go of the fireman pole early, and otherwise making my own rules. But if it's one thing I've learned in tag, it's that jumping is faster. Faster keeps me from being "it," which keeps me from running around trying to catch kids that are faster than I am. Steven is on the top step. I'm going to vault the purple arm bars.

Just as I'm about to jump, I see Kayla running through the woodchips below, chasing some boy. I would have squashed her. But I really have no time now. If it isn't the wind, I can feel Steven's breath on me. All of the kids on the playground are screaming, talking, laughing. I have to jump now, or I'll be "it."

Normally, it's a short fall and I can hit the ground running or in a roll. But today it's a long fall. Because Kayla appears out of the chaos and the crowd and she is right underneath me. I might still miss her if I can move backwards.

All goes wrong. I move back too far and my left leg connects with a large beam of wood. When I do meet the ground, it's not wood chips I feel. I've landed on Kayla anyway. Feeling dumb, guilty, and mostly terrified, I scoot off of her.

"Are you okay? Are you alright? I'm sorry!"

But she's already sprung up and is dusting herself off.

"Yeah, I'm fine."

I'm astonished, but relieved. Kayla is about half my size.

Kayla tries to help me up, and all of a sudden everything is wrong again. The rest of the tag kids are coming in slowly and as Kayla edges away they watch me trying to walk. My right foot seems to be doing fine, but every time I take a step with my left foot, I am in more pain.

"Damn!"

Mike comes up to me, asking if I'm alright. The dolphin on his Miami jacket looks sad.

"I don't know..." I respond, still testing it. I can feel wood chips sliding into my shoe, but for once this is the least of my worries.

"Don't worry about it. Just shake it off, and let's play some tag already."

"I don't think I can, my foot hurts too much."

Mike looks disappointed, but not half as disheartened as I feel. Maybe it will take care of itself and I'll be at it again in a day or two. But as I watch Steven, Mike, and the rest of the kids going back to their game, running around in the last minutes of the recess sun, something in the back of my mind tells me I probably won't be playing tag any time soon.

THE PERKS OF IMPRISONMENT

To a kid, a broken ankle is just as bad as a death sentence. Immediately upon realizing there was something really wrong with my ankle, I went into a denial of sorts (made much worse by my infamous pain tolerance). I remembered the couple of weeks or so that an enlarged spleen put me out of commission as a kid, recalled the insane discipline and parental scolding necessary to keep me from running during visits to the park or running and sliding down the banister. As I hobbled off the playground that day, what scared me was not the thought of the weeks on crutches but the removal from my normal recess activities. How long would it be before I could join my newfound group again?

Even though I tried to downplay my injury, Mom was terrified to hear what had happened to me when the school contacted her.

"I think something's wrong with my ankle; it feels funny," I had told them.

When she retells the story to others, Mom always makes it a point to mention that my ankle had swollen up to the size of a softball. It's no wonder that Mom used to keep me home from school whenever I complained about so much as a minor headache. My pain threshold is very high to begin with, and when I do start to feel pain I try to ignore it. Just a few more days of this (sickness, ankle pain, throbbing in my lower back), and it will probably go away, I reason with myself. I won't have to worry anyone, but most importantly, I won't have to deal with the anxiety of a routine change. I won't have to waste an entire afternoon at the doctor's or stay home from school and have to make up an impossible amount of back work. It was only when Mom brought the swelling to my attention that I really started to get worried about my own well-being. But as we waited to be seen in the hospital, it wasn't my ankle that I worried about when I asked Mom over and over again whether or not she thought my ankle was broken. It was broken in two places, we were told. I left with an air cast, a couple of wooden crutches, and a four-week sentence.

Because I viewed even slight changes in routine as apocalyptic events, the idea that my broken ankle might in fact serve me in some way or even become a blessing in disguise was far from my mind. Like most people, I still have trouble seeing the bright side when things just don't go right for me. Though uncoordinated, I was very active as a child. My sister and I had always hiked, biked, and ran ourselves directly into the tantrum stage of tired whenever the opportunity presented itself. I liked school—and it was actually around this time that I really started to realize I was good at it—but welcomed the recess break in my day as any kid does. I didn't realize at the time that lunch was not only my time to exercise, but my only hour of the day to focus entirely on experiments with socialization. I would wait for another few long years before learning to step back outside of my own life to become aware of the illusion that there are good events and bad events.

That I was dreading my virtual imprisonment isn't to say I didn't notice some perks of my condition fairly immediately. For one, I could get people to do things for me. Not that I have ever been one who is thrilled by the idea of ordering people around, but everyone deserves some service every once in a while. More attractive to me, however, was being able to spend hours on end reading. In my time of immobility, I devoured as many

Goosebumps books as I possibly could. I remember being stricken by the whopping two hundred or so pages contained by each book. That someone could sit down and write one of these, let alone dozens, amazed me. So, it was around this time that I first decided I'd start to try and take my ambitions as a writer seriously. My first story was a sixteen-pager that boiled down to five typed pages. The title escapes me, but it detailed a father and son's creepy camping trip. As RL Stine was my greatest influence at the time, the story starts close to the good part and ended with what I considered to be an impressive twist (the identity of the werewolf was, gasp, the boy's father). When I was done writing that story, I decided I would start something more serious. Real writers wrote longer books, so that's what I would do.

My mom always encouraged my writing and was the exact right combination of proud of and amused by me. When we visited her friends (some of whom were mothers of kids who had gone to physical or occupational therapy at the same time as me) or my sister's friends, Mom would say:

"Tell Mrs. V about what you're working on!"

"What I'm working on?" I'd reply, confused. *Nothing right now, I'm standing here with you*, would be the first thing I'd think.

"You know, your next writing project," she'd elaborate.

"Ohh. Yeah, I'm going to write a book. It's going to be at least fifty pages!"

Writing a book would be difficult, I knew. I wasn't sure I had any one-hundred-and-fifty-page ideas yet, so I set my goals a bit lower than I wanted to. But I had my ambitions and what I thought was an important perspective. I liked Stine's writing, but hadn't it been a while since he was a kid? My characters that were kids would be more realistic, as I was still a kid myself.

"I have a crush on so-and-so, but I'd never admit it," Stine's characters often reported, for example. I, on the other hand, was starting to know what it was like to have a crush on someone. But even in my fourth and fifth grade days, it wasn't that I would never admit it to them. My obstacle was communication; I simply didn't know how to talk to them. What's more, my new story would actually be scary. I wanted it to be taken seriously, so I decided I would write something that wasn't necessarily for kids, but from the point of view of a kid.

INTO THE WRITING WORLD

Dad and Laura have gone for a walk around the pond, leaving me to sit at this wooden bench under the shade of a large tree. Those weird rusted grills are all about, but I don't trust them. Dad always brings his own, portable propane grill. When they've disappeared under the willows, the park feels that much emptier. I gaze over at my crutches. Cold, wooden, and smelling of rubber, these things will be leaving imprints on my armpits for another few weeks or so yet. I want to hate them. I kind of do hate them, but some part of me realizes it's only my immobility that I'm hating.

"You're a big kid, and let's face it, not the most coordinated. You really have to be more careful; you might not be able to do all of the things that the other kids do," Mom told me. Even after I heal, teachers and monitors will be hounding me not to jump off of the top of things anymore. But just because I hurt myself once doesn't mean I'm not smart enough to make sure it doesn't happen again. I am already growing tired of commanding the extra attention afforded by having my own communication notebook for my mom and my teachers (none of the other kids have to have those!).

That's why, even though the park feels empty, I'm completely comfortable here. I feel the same way when I'm sitting down with a book. Reading is something I can do on my own. It's only me and the words here—no conversations to enter, no "indoor voice," no worries about interruptions. Writing is the same way. Lately, I've been interested in taking that fun, thrilled, and scared feeling I get from reading and hearing horror stories and creating it in stories myself. But for all of my imagination, creating stories out of ideas is quite a bit trickier even than I would have thought.

I forget my challenges and just look around me. The geese are honking in the distance, probably because Dad and Laura are speed-walking by. Beyond the pine trees, the river flows and babbles loudly. The willows that dot the path of Otsiningo Park sway slightly in the wind. Underneath them, lamp posts sit unlit.

It's the lamp post that transports me to that place. A little patch of light surrounded by darkness. I thought of those dramatic neighborhood watch signs with the guy in the Carmen Sandiego trench coat and low-pulled hat often hung on those types of lamp posts. A real bad guy wouldn't care about any silly neighborhood watch sign. Really terrifying villains don't care whether or not someone is watching them. I bet there are people, probably the scariest sort, who can get past even the most advanced security systems.

I can feel myself getting sucked more and more into the three subject notebook, away from the world of dogs on leashes, people jogging, biking, rollerblading, moving. In my mind it is summer. With a few changes, the neighborhood I lived in as a young child becomes the setting for the story. My character sits in front of the television with his parents on a hot summer day. There's a story on the news about a fiendish killer. My character doesn't know anyone is in danger; his father invents home security systems. Boy, does he have a surprise coming. I let myself drift the way I'm accustomed to. I stare off into space, still receiving information from the outside world but receding farther into the world of the story. Sometimes it's when I stare into the paper, in the middle of getting another line down, that the next scene or line of dialogue enters my thoughts. At times, a jarring noise or an obstacle in my plot will tear me from my work and I'll check the path for signs of Dad or Laura. By the time they come back around the loop— my dad trying to keep up with Laura, both of them sweating, the sun lower in the sky—I don't want to leave.

"Are you ready bud?" Dad asks.

"Here, I'll carry your notebook for you, but hurry up, I want to get dessert. We have to be back to Mom's soon."

Mom's. Crap. I've completely forgotten about time. It's a Dad night, but we still have to be home by eight. If it weren't for that stupid (damn) accident on the playground, I would have been able to walk around the pond with Dad and hiss at the geese with

Laura. But as the change in routine becomes my new routine, I mind less and less.

As I hop to the car (and I'm actually getting pretty good at working these bulky crutches) I think about my situation. Sure, it would have been nice to get exercise, although Mom is already making comments about how the crutches are giving me Popeye forearms. As I get into Dad's old Chevy truck and pull the crutches in after myself, I realize I'm grateful for the time to myself so that I can write. I will later find that people call the feeling I got at the park being "in the flow," or "in the zone." But it will be some time before I learn that my autistic ability to go off into my own world isn't just an obstacle I have to overcome. It's a doorway into an area of intense power, creativity, strangeness, and concentration.

THE CIRCUS CLASS

It was right around fourth grade that I can remember starting to enter in any sort of social circle. Second grade had been a transition year, but third grade had been very awkward. While I excelled in school, moving straight to third grade English, I gained little ground on the social front. I got along with some of the kids in my class, but it's difficult to think of one person I would have called a good friend during that time, except of course for my sister. When I got an unmarked Valentine that read "I love you, Dylan," I incorrectly assumed and was conned into believing that Melissa, a girl who rode the bus home with me every day, had written it. I was excited, but had a feeling of being kept in the dark, missing the big picture of what was happening.

"She goes out with guys and breaks up with them just for fun," I was warned. So after my mom said something to the effect of "third graders don't go out with fourth graders in my book," I was incredibly aggravated to not be able to make my own decision in the matter, but even more annoyed when she did just what I was told she would.

Miss Amaria's class was the closest thing to a stereotypical circus classroom I can think of. I can remember the young teacher smiling, in front of the window, dividing up the classroom.

"Cal, Kayla, Franky, Brian, Angelo...and Dylan, stand over there. The rest of you over there. Now when I say go, cheer!"

We cheered, letting loose banshee wails that would have terrified specters themselves. We easily put the other side of the class to shame.

"Now look," Miss Amaria said, laughing in spite of herself. "These four are outshouting all of the rest of you. Let's have more enthusiasm."

It was the only time I can remember her asking us to get rowdier. Probably, this was a major reason I really felt I was an outsider as a temporary cripple. Our games of mum-ball got so intense that people regularly fell out of desks. On one occasion, a ball hit someone's head and flew out the window. On another, the tennis ball bounced off of Angelo's head, onto the ceiling, and onto Angelo's head again before anyone knew what to do about it. Another student, Brian, was always giving Miss Amaria and the aide, Mrs. Mulranny, trouble. His escapades included taunting people and then over-dramatizing the situation until he had dragged the teacher, the aide, and several classmates into an arguing match. They often had to chase him around and out of the classroom, and he would then stand at the door smiling and pressing his nearly bald head against the window as Miss Amaria shook her bangs away from her face and told us to ignore him. She often had to wrangle Franky, who had a penchant for teasing, rowdy behavior, and play-fights. Franky was the only kid in class who was as tall as me (our mutual tallness was one of the reasons I originally approached Franky in the first place). Though at the time I didn't think my broken ankle was doing me any favors, despite the time I had to read and write, it actually lent me a hand at a very important time.

ATTEMPTS AT BEING APPROPRIATE

"After you," Cal says. I can't tell if he's having trouble holding the large metal door open or if he's shaking because he just doesn't like to stand still. Either way, I hobble into the room as quickly as I can.

"Dylan, slow down on those, you're going to fall," Mrs. Mulranny calls. I get the same feeling of a rush to my head that I get whenever I'm corrected by an adult.

"Sorry," I mutter, not making eye contact. I slide into my seat and prop the crutches onto the seat next to mine where no one is sitting. While by back was turned, Cal has already gotten his notebook together on his desk and is coming towards me with mine, which I had had with me at lunch. He's short with red, spiky hair and glasses. I think of him as my opposite sometimes, walking next to me or ahead of me down the hall. I am proud of my tallness, but I don't look down on Cal. I am noticing in Cal a personality trait I'll covet well into high school. He talks to everyone. He makes Kayla, the cutest girl in class, laugh. He hangs around with Franky. I don't know one kid in class that Cal doesn't get along with. I want to be like that. I want to make Kayla laugh.

"Here you go," Cal says. He's practically back to his own desk and chattering back there before I can comment.

"Thank you, so much, Cal for helping Dylan out," Miss Amaria says.

"No problem!" Cal replies. Years later he will tell me that being able to go to lunch early with me was a major motivation for helping me out all of the time, though even now that revelation won't have made the situation feel any less fortuitous. Cal will be my first best friend.

"Alright! We didn't get around to them yesterday, so I'm carving out some time right now. Get out your journals. Some of you already have them out, good. Brian, I am warning you. I'm going to give you a few minutes, and write about whatever you want to."

Aside from lunch, journals are my favorite time of day. My mind races with all of the different possibilities. I stare into the far reaches of the blackboard, the metal chalk tray, the white, slightly pop-corned wall. I won't work on "Perfect Murder on Elm Street." I want to do something new. I want to do something really scary. Maybe it will be something to do with werewolves. I concentrate, fidgeting with my pencil. Didn't I tell a scary story on the road back from Cortland one evening with my dad? I love telling stories at night, watching the trees go by in the darkness.

The road is a scary place! Especially if you had to pull over, and if the woods were filled with evil things, like werewolves… I get lost in the writing until my fingers start to hurt. I don't have strong fingers, I'm told. That's why sometimes I have to take a break from writing and do some special stretches a physical therapist showed me. Miss Amaria's voice interrupts me as I'm trying to bring my last scene to a close.

"Time is up! Alright, who wants to share?"

I never feel like I have enough time in writing exercises. Everyone else is done, but I'm still writing. That's how I feel when Mrs. Mulranny has to re-copy what I've written because my hand writing is so unclear. I'm outside in the hall, still stuck on the test while everyone moves on. It's the same feeling I get when I'm in the car or walking somewhere and I know that I will be late.

No one's hand has gone up yet, so I put my pencil down and throw mine into the air.

"Okay, Dylan."

I start reading my story about a van that is found on the side of the road with the radio still going. The police found it the next morning with the doors open, and a man's intestines spread over the back of the car—

"That's enough, Dylan. That's just too gory for class today. Anyone else?"

I'm stunned. Usually, the teacher loves my journals and wants to hear them. Usually, she compliments my writing. I go red in the face and shut my book. I can hear Cal, Franky, Angelo, and others laughing behind me. I should have thought of that, but I still think that I should be able to write what I want. The teacher did say we could write whatever we wanted. I guess that wasn't the whole truth.

"Alright, Krista."

"Ying," Angelo screeches from the back of the room. Usually, Mrs. Mulranny or Miss Amaria will reprimand him, but they either don't hear him or are ignoring him. He says "ying" all of the time.

"Ying."

There it is again. It's one of the things he keeps going back to. Angelo is chubby, wears glasses, and is just plain weird. He rants about chickens, turkeys, and Nintendo. It drives me crazy, and he knows it. His refrain is endless, behind me.

"Ignore it!" is the advice I get when it comes to my sister doing something annoying or someone else "trying to get my goat" as Mom says. I always thought that was a strange phrase, and I am still not sure why it is used to mean intentionally trying to get a reaction out of someone. I understand that not every expression makes logical sense. We spend a lot of time in speech class going over idioms. I'll realize later that I understand a lot more about expressions that shouldn't be taken literally than I was getting credit for. I'm just not great at communicating that.

"Angelo, cut it out," Mrs. Mulranny whispers. Her voice is close by, and I did not even notice her move to the back of the room.

As Krista starts to read, her thick Ukrainian accent weighing heavily on my attention, I glance back at Angelo. He is still scowling—apparently he doesn't like being told he's doing something wrong, either. When he sees me looking, though, his face contorts to a smile so exaggerated, it looks vicious. I laugh, even though I know Krista is still reading and that it's rude to interrupt. It has always been difficult for me not to interrupt when I feel that whatever's going on in my mind is more important than whatever's going on in the real world. The mutual, forbidden laugh we shared (the first of many to come) seems a significant moment to me, for some reason.

SEEDS OF FRIENDSHIP

I was expecting Easter morning to go terribly. I have crutches and Laura does not. Of course she will find more eggs and therefore get more candy than me. But Grandma Godwin is down to visit, and she keeps yelling at Laura to make sure she leaves some for me, and of course she does. I always appreciated it, but have learned gradually what a good sister Laura has always been to me. As I stumbled and slipped from room to room with Mom yelling from another room to make sure I slowed down, I could see Laura's slender fingers itching to dart out and pick up every egg, but she held back.

Easter morning in fourth grade is the last memory I have of living with the crutches. When my air cast came off I was still condemned to two weeks of walking rather than running. When that time was up, I remember feeling like a prisoner released from my bonds. I really felt it for Steven, whom I didn't play with much anymore. His feet were in braces almost all of the time, and the way he walked, it didn't look like he had any respite.

As the gates of the playground were opened to me once again, I felt the world of social circles starting to piece itself together in my head. Whether or not I realized it at the time, I very much used Cal as a role model. Cal is what I would call a floater. Even in fourth grade, and despite his shortness and glasses which might otherwise have rendered him geeky, Cal was friends with just about everyone. He lived near and was friends with Steven as well as most other people in the class. As the years drew on, Cal seemed to amass even more friends and acquaintances. Whenever we walked down a hall together, he slapped hands with several people I didn't know.

Instead of playing tag, I played kickball or football. I didn't fully learn football until I played it every day in middle school, so I always had to ask what was going on. Even though I wasn't contributing much to my fourth and fifth grade lunch-time teams, it felt good to be a part of something. For some reason, I liked kickball a lot better. I'm not sure I ever kicked a home run, but I caught a few balls to get opposing teammates out and I rounded the bases home a few times.

Even more valuable to me was probably the time I had to just sit around in the shade by the back fence and talk.

I once saw Kayla talking to Franky. Franky departed, lumbering past me without even a word. As of that point, we'd had at least a couple of conversations mainly detailing the basic stuff (his favorite animal was the eagle while mine was a tiger), so I didn't quite understand why he didn't want to talk to me.

"What's wrong with Franky?" I asked Kayla. We stood by the rusting fence, through which trees were growing, giving us valuable shade.

"It's...nothing," she told the ground, kicking at it. I didn't like giving eye contact too much, but still looked for it in other people. I suppose I'm still a bit like that.

"Well, what did you say to him?" I hadn't quite come to understand the difference in showing interest in other peoples' lives and prying too deeply for knowledge that may be too personal. But she stopped kicking at the blacktop, looked up at me briefly, and I knew I was close.

"Just...Franky likes me and I like him. He's really funny. But my dad is a racist. He doesn't like black people, and I just told Franky that we can't go out."

I was so stunned that I didn't know what to say. I really had asked to know too much, but once she got started telling me, I could tell it felt good. Come to think of it, this is the first experience I had of talking successfully to a member of the opposite sex. I'm not sure when kids are supposed to start getting interested in girls. To me, it seems I had always held some level of interest in girls. I watched a home movie of myself from kindergarten. I come off of the bus (a long one, not the short bus I would be ridiculed for riding in elementary school) and immediately started talking to my mom about Brittany, the most beautiful girl in the class. I have always considered myself at somewhat of a disadvantage when it comes to talking to girls, but I do have one redeeming quality which has saved me time again. It turns out, even for my lack of communication skills, that I'm a good listener. I may not be looking the speaker in the eye (although I've gotten much better at holding eye contact) but I am hearing every word they say. I eventually learned to unplug myself from the track of my own thoughts, speech, and interest and wonder at the lives of others. I discovered that the same ear I had for remembering and impersonating voices, and the same ear which helped me to learn other languages, helped me to listen in a way that is thorough and deep.

At this time, Cal was the only one in school I could call a true friend. I would slowly become friends with Franky as we'd be in the same class with Cal and Angelo the next year. Despite my ability to listen (and probably because I, you know, fell on her once), I only hung around and spoke to Kayla when I was with Cal. As for Angelo, I wasn't ready to be friends with him yet. He certainly liked to talk to me a lot, but his lack of regard for just how odd he acted and how weirdly he came across disconcerted me. There was something very abrasive about his nature. I wouldn't have wanted to admit that we were similar, each with vocabularies including a steady stream of non sequiturs and both having difficulty getting along with others. We were the smart, weird kids—last to be picked for dodgeball, but the last two up at the board racing each other to get to the end of math problems when all of the others had long since stopped trying. Perhaps I didn't want to see that, like Angelo, I was far from feeling like I knew where I belonged, or that I belonged at all. But I had sown some important seeds that would prove important to my future growth.

CHAPTER 6

REGULAR PEOPLE

I'm in a familiar place—high above the playground, climbing on what looks like a fireman's pole, but twisted up on itself.

"Hey, get down from there, monkey boy!"

Who's calling me a monkey? Isn't it normal for a kid to climb on a playground? I look down, and standing below me is Cameron.

I know Cameron from my days at Johnson City—he's a friend of mine, so he must be kidding. I hesitate, making a quick assessment on whether or not anyone else is down there, and jump to join him. I brace myself for the impact, but my ankle has long since healed, and woodchips scatter harmlessly. It's nearing time to go inside, and we catch up on the way.

"What class are you in?" he asks me as we head up the giant stone staircase up to school. I answer that I have Mrs. Ashton, and am disappointed when he says he has some other teacher, and have to part ways once we gain entrance to the building. Climbing up the four flights of stairs to my new classroom, I realize something weird. This building is feeling old to me now. It's far from the hulking, alien brick structure I first encountered when I set foot in here a few years ago. Instead, I seem to know what's going to be on every bulletin board. I know which steps are going to be busted. I know the fastest route anywhere in the building.

I'm on the last flight of stairs to my new classroom, and I can hear the voices of my future classmates mixing together in the hall. I can't see them yet, and for some reason I all of a sudden have a strange desire to simply turn around and walk away. What if I don't want this? Sure, I'm ready. I have all of the school supplies I could need, and before I left, Mom made sure I had my notebook with her note for my new teacher and that

I knew where my classroom is. But what if Mrs. Ashton isn't as nice as Miss Amaria? Miss A saved my butt a couple of times when I spoke out of turn in the middle of class and was supposed to go to detention. I think she knew it was hard for me to keep my mouth shut sometimes and I'm working on it. What if Mrs. Ashton is less understanding?

And it's not only Mrs. Ashton I am worried about. I know that fifth grade is the last year before I head to middle school. The years themselves all seemed long, but looking back the time has passed more quickly than I thought. What if I finish the fifth grade and I'm still not ready for the middle school? I hear that the middle school is huge. It's hard to find your way around. My team of teachers will prepare us by having us take math and English with different teachers, so that we have to switch classrooms like the middle school kids do.

I'm already nearing the last step. The staircase has gone by much faster than I remember. The group of students is huddled outside of a door labeled "Mrs. Ashton," so I know I am in the right place. I've been in this hallway before, hanging out after lunch. I remember I was talking to a fifth grader who also claimed to like to eat a lot. I was quite disappointed; he wasn't impressed when I told him I could eat an entire pizza, huge burgers, and ten pancakes. He kept telling me *that's nothing.* Now *I'm* the fifth grader. I repeat that to myself a few times to let it sink in, the same way I do with birthdays, so I can get used to the new number in my head. There are few things more embarrassing than giving the wrong answer when someone asks you how old you are or what grade you are in.

There are actually quite a few kids from Miss Amaria's class here, and that comforts me. I can pick out Cal's spiky hair and the glint of his glasses and the shine of Franky's bald head above everyone else's. Angelo is standing there, too. He isn't acting all crazy for now; he's just tucked away into the world of his Game Boy.

"Ying!" he says when he sees me, and immediately goes back to the game. Tran, one of the two Vietnamese boys I approached on my first day at this school, turns around, but quickly returns to speaking with this kid with a huge afro. I have a cold feeling in my stomach accompanied by a slight cold tingling up my back. I am embarrassed for him. Doesn't he know that could be offensive? I am also feeling latent embarrassment for when I came up to them assuming they were Japanese.

There are also a lot of kids from the other fourth grade classes and some kids I haven't seen at all, even on the playground. One of them has brown hair that turns bright yellow on top. I think it looks funny, but he has an earring—a gold stud like mine. In third grade, I really wanted an earring, and to my surprise, Mom let me have one, which I was thrilled with because I was sure it would make me look cool. Maybe the earring will give me something to talk with this kid about.

But I'll get to that another time. I'm going to stick with talking to kids I already know.

"Well what do you know?" I ask in a voice reminiscent of a cartoon detective who has come upon a clue. It has the desired effect and Cal jumps. He turns around and gives me a high five.

As the bell rings, my new teacher, who is tall with medium-length black hair and intense eyes, opens the door and hurries us into the classroom, telling us to quiet down.

"Hey, if you break your ankle this year, I'm not going to help carry your books for a month this time," Cal says.

"Huh? I don't *think* I will…" But he's smiling. Too late, I've realized he's kidding.

The new classroom isn't big, it isn't menacing. It's different; the chalkboard is facing a different way, and so are the windows. But the aide, Mrs. Bocelli, is very nice and I get the feeling it may not be so bad this year. Angelo is sitting behind me, taunting me with "Chicken!" But I can smile. I've kind of gotten used to it.

THE TRANSFORMATION BEGINS

I remember thinking: it is no coincidence that they are teaching us sexual education right now. Sure, I remembered the one or two introductory classes we sat through in fourth grade. But they only skimmed the surface, telling me things I already knew, such as that one could get an erection staring at the map of the United States, and not just when aroused.

During my fourth grade year, Mom was teaching fifth grade at a Catholic school in the area. My sister was especially mad, having been taken from her Catholic school and introduced into a public elementary school. As it turns out I am not the only Emmons child to be opposed to routine. But at one point during the year, I remember there was some type of sexual education book for kids on the dining room table, complete with comical, nonhuman characters. I correctly assumed that it was a part of my mom's teaching materials.

Whenever I found myself alone in the room, I would flip through the pages quickly. But I would always be on my guard. I didn't want to be surprised by anyone—that would be far too embarrassing. One day, I found the book left open. Had I done that? I read the page intermittently as I walked by, until I had a few moments alone with it. It explained that sex was something that happened when a man and a woman got close, and went into the details of just how close.

Previously, I had just known that sex was something that happened when people were naked and kissing. No matter how much I thought about it, I couldn't wrap my head around the significance of the fact that all of the changes I would see in the next few years had this as the ultimate goal.

I found it weird that all of my sex education in school had in mind the anxiety and dread that came with bodily changes. I was strangely okay with this. I was ready to transform into a bigger, better, more interesting person. I understood that puberty was something that happened when people got older, but I found some comfort in the fact that we all had to go through it at the same time. Maybe this is one reason I hadn't yet morphed into the angsty and impatient teenager I would shortly become.

We were all in the same boat, all of the boys and girls. I knew it was no coincidence, because I saw all of the changes happening around me. Some of my male classmates would find ways to make a big deal about newfound armpit hair or brag about deodorant use. Some girls had sprouted breasts practically overnight—it was impossible not to notice.

There was something delightfully awkward about sitting in a room with all of my buddies, listening to two male teachers talking about puberty and sex. We stifled our snickering while Mr. Kelly and Mr. Hutch spoke about private parts in the same tone of voice they usually spoke about math.

After some time, the team stopped their talk. They passed out index cards and urged us to take this last part of the class seriously. At each little table, the four or five of us would have a chance to write down questions anonymously to be answered. Even as an eleven-year-old I had a feeling this would lead to some less-than-serious and less-than-appropriate answers. Like the others, I had to try earnestly to mask my apprehension and excitement with bathroom humor and a giddy laugh. But I was actually curious, and found myself slightly annoyed when a kid at my table slid an index card towards Mr. Kelly and immediately started snickering. Jake always smelled a bit funny and made it a point to fart and sneeze audibly. His question would surely be good for laughs, but probably not for much else.

"Here's one: 'Is it true that you're not a man until you have sex with a woman?'"

Some of the guys howled at that one, including Jake. Among the laughs, I could pick out Angelo's and Franky's easily. But I was surprised—most of us stayed silent, kept our composure. Like me, I'm sure they were waiting to hear how the teachers would respond. Mr. Kelly was very careful and, I now realize, probably stifling a laugh when he answered.

"No. Puberty happens and you become a man regardless of whether or not you have sex with a woman. What about priests and other people who don't have sex? They're men, aren't they?"

Of course the teacher was right. I had no idea that in the space of a few years I'd again be wondering at the answer to Jake's question. But then, my mind was focused on different questions. Was there a girl sitting in Mrs. Ashton's room writing an equally preposterous question on some index card? What would Alicia be wondering?

Alicia sat in front of me in Mrs. Ashton's, right in front of the chalkboard. I couldn't say what it was that drew me to her. On the occasions we spoke, I looked over her thick, brown curls and her big smile. I wanted to be around her; I wanted her to like me. When we switched seats to make groups in class I scrambled to get to her seat and feel its warmth. Yet when she hugged me once, saying "Hey, my Dylan!" I stood in her arms, frozen and wondering what to do. Most, including my own mother, misinterpreted me. It wasn't that I despised contact with other people. The feeling of her pressed against me and squeezing was alarming, but not altogether unpleasant. It didn't trigger my mild claustrophobia. But it was like my thoughts were clogging up my neuropaths so that I could hardly move at all. I was having an Asperger's freeze, which is what I call it when I find myself in an unfolding situation and can't react for a few moments.

I would later write in my journal of the joy of an early summertime trip to the park during which I was fortunate enough to witness Alicia's swimsuit malfunction. I wondered aloud on the page how it was that parents let their daughters run around half-naked (not that I was complaining). I wrote down all of the things I felt when she flirtatiously asked me to "save her" and had me drag her out of the deep water. Most importantly, though, I wrote about the fact that Alicia was going out with Tony, who I thought was trying way too hard to be a badass. It wasn't his bleached hair or earring that made me judge him—I'd have both at one point or another. It was his attitude. As someone who hated conflict, I had a problem deciphering the logic of someone so quick to rage. And I had a hell of a time wondering why a girl like her was drawn to a dude like him.

These thoughts and wanderings crossed paths in my journal with subjects like the beginning of *Wild Wild West*, the erotic situation and partial nudity of which seemed to have me itching from the inside out. Also held within the pages are my reflections on my own frustrations at going cross-country skiing for the first time with Dad and Laura.

"G*D D*** these skis," I censored myself. Even at that age, I understood that my own frustrated reactions to having to learn something new were limiting my potential. I reflected that I had actually had quite a good time when I calmed down and started to enjoy nature. Writing a journal was as much an adventure as it was semi-therapeutic, but it was important in turning my writing inward. As I do not always have the skill to work out my thoughts in conversation or amidst the other worker bees buzzing around my brain, writing became an important medium for me. Though I had hardly realized it, I had started to become fascinated with trying to figure myself out on the page. The personal essay (or autobiographical fiction, poetry, etc.) has a way of giving me an outside perspective on my life and my world.

Chapter 7

TRANSITIONS

We grow up in unexpected ways. Some things, like my impending transition into middle school, crash down on us like waves and sweep us into new areas of our lives. But we do wish for the illusion of choice when it comes to the things we experience which really have the potential to change us. Of the activities I became involved in, some, such as chorus and piano lessons, stand in my mind as gambles or educated guesses that ended up working. It turns out the ear that helps me with impersonations and foreign languages also picks up on music.

I think that one of the reasons I ended up enjoying Karate was because it was my choice, my interest, and my decision. I had tried martial arts on a few previous occasions, but I had been nowhere near as mature as I would have needed to be to excel in martial arts.

I remember standing in a room at the YMCA doing punches. Though the instructor wanted me to look towards the front of the room, my gaze wandered to the room's many mirrors.

"Keep looking ahead and stop saying 'I want to go home,'" the instructor reprimanded me several times.

"Do I have to sit on my knees?" I asked in the middle of my first and last class at another place.

"Yes, as long as your legs aren't broken," the black belt in the front of the room responded.

I tried Karate again when I was eleven. My mom had chosen Winding River (so named for the Susquehanna River, one of two that run through Binghamton) because she had heard good things about the instructor. Supposedly, he was very good with kids, even those with learning disabilities. Over my five years of training and assisting with classes there, those who had recommended Winding River would be proven right several times over. I can remember at least two other autistic kids who trained under Master Sterling and excelled in the program that would see me evolve from an uncoordinated and frustrated but driven student into a competent assistant instructor. I can think of few other things I've been a part of that have so marked my transition into manhood.

ON MARTIAL ARTS AND ACHIEVING GOALS

The building is white with a huge window through which the people driving on Front Street can see people in white uniforms taking class. It's strange to see the same window that I've passed so many times from the inside, but this view isn't as interesting. On the other side of Front Street is a wall that hides the Susquehanna from view. Next to it is an old building that clearly no longer produces the ice the sign advertises. In the far right corner of the window and almost out of view hovers a billboard that will try to suck up my attention with beer ads and public service announcements (PSAs).

Having just walked in, I stand with Mom for a moment and assess the studio. I have the strange sense of confusion and wonder that I get when I try to reconcile reality with my expectations. The school isn't as big as I would have expected. The training floor is green, and right now it stands empty. At the head of the room, the South Korean and American flags hang side by side, split by the photo of a man I will come to know as the Grand Master. Three rows of plastic chairs wait for parents to drop kids off at class.

A man with glasses and a brisk walk comes out of one of the offices, shaking hands and talking to my mom first. They must have spoken over the phone. He shakes my hand and introduces himself as Mr. Fuller. My first thought as I follow him to the locker room with my uniform still in its bag is that this guy doesn't look much like a Karate instructor. He helps me learn how to tie the top, which needs two shoelace knots in weird places.

"This is the first of two private lessons you'll get before you start going to regular classes. Are you ready?"

I nod. We are standing in a miniature training room behind the offices and next to the women's locker room. The sun is shining brightly, directly on my face. Is this going to be hard?

"How high do you think you can kick?" Mr. Fuller asks me after some warm ups.

"I don't know…maybe here?" I raise my hand to about chest level. Is this the right answer? What's he getting at?

"Right there? Okay, let's try it out. The first kick we're going to try is what we call the front stretch kick."

He demonstrates, bending his front knee and straightening the other out behind him in a front stance, then swinging his back leg up, unbent. I give it a try, and he has to remind me to keep my leg bent. Another try, and he reminds me to bring my leg back to where it started after I kick. This reminds me of the ax kick I learned from a brief martial arts class at summer camp; I asked the teacher there what belt he had. He was only a purple belt, and I could tell he was offended that I asked and was disappointed. I haven't dared to ask Mr. Fuller what his rank is.

He picks up a pad that he straps to his hand and holds in front of me. I swing my leg up and hit the pad.

"Good!" he says, and moves the pad higher. I kick higher and hit it again. He moves it up a third time and I don't think about it, I just kick.

"Good!" he practically screams.

I look at him quizzically.

"You just kicked over your head."

I did?

He holds his now empty hand a few inches above my head, where I apparently just had my foot. Does this mean I might be good at Karate?

"This represents a philosophy of martial arts and Soo Bahk Do. We set goals for ourselves, increase them little by little, and we might even surprise ourselves."

LIVING IN TWO WORLDS

I have some goals in mind. This may not be so bad; I'm not begging to go home, nor is the instructor yelling at me. By the end of my next class, if all goes well, I will have my white belt. On our way out, I catch something I missed earlier. On the wall across from the windows, above the mirrors, is a long line of framed pictures. In each is a man or a woman wearing a uniform with midnight-blue trim. I nod at them on my way out the door. I'll be up there on that wall someday. What I don't realize is the impossible amount of discipline it will take for me to get there, or how much I will have changed before I'm through.

LOOKING FORWARD

Reading my fifth grade journal, you'd never know I was nervous to transition into middle school.

I alone (with the exception of [my speech therapist] Mrs. Edwards) am going to visit West Middle for a day this week. It is to help me make the transition easier and Mom and a few others have been talking about it for a long time. I am looking forward to going there next year for a number of reasons. For one, the lunches are big and so is the school. Two, there are a lot of people there and some hot girls. I hope to get a serious girlfriend and go on some dates. Mom says there are going to be a lot of dances and activities to go to. And there, the classes will be harder and it will be different altogether.

The journal entry detailing my first trip to West Middle mainly highlights the lunch options ("You can have the lunch ladies make you your personalized deli sandwich with anything on it that you like. They have hot lunch and pizza every day!"). To be fair, I was excited for the opportunity to eat big lunches, take harder classes, and meet a lot of girls. But the large building intimidated me more than I'd admit to myself even in the pages of a private notebook.

Another thing that intimidated me was that I was having trouble figuring out the girl I decided I liked. Alicia was a mystery to me. It seemed that one day she would hug me and call me her best buddy, and the next she'd ignore me. It could have had something to do with the fact that my first reaction to a hug wasn't to hug back, but to simply stand there. When I think about it, I must have been quite the mystery myself.

CHAPTER 8

INCLUSION

Home on break during my second year of my undergraduate studies, I walked on up to the counter at Main Street Hollywood Video and handed my movie to the girl at the register. She was cute, and I hadn't seen her there before. Still, I wasn't expecting much of an encounter; maybe I'd make some small talk about the movie I had picked out or the weather before I was sent on my merry way with *The Evil Dead* and a due date. If I was lucky, I could get her talking a little, since it was a slow night. But after she learned my name and number, she stopped and smiled.

"I think we went to summer camp together at the Heritage, do you remember?"

"Yeah, I went there," I paused, taking a look down at her nametag. "Audrey! Holy shit! I'm surprised you remembered. That was a long time ago."

"I thought I recognized you!"

We stood at the counter for a few minutes catching up a little. It was somewhat unreal, but then again Binghamton isn't a huge town. Inevitably, a customer came up behind me and I quickly asked her if she was on Facebook. Yes, she was.

I friend-requested her later that night, but we've hardly spoken since; she got married, and the store shut down years ago. But the chance meeting had gotten me thinking, rewinding about a decade to my time spent under the sun at the Heritage.

The Heritage Country Club in Vestal, New York was a typical one—golf course, dining room, etc. But in the summer, it hosted a day camp for kids up to twelve and thirteen. All of the staples of a day camp were there—sports, minimal arts and crafts, swimming, organized activities, camp food, and mainly teenage counselors. The majority of campers came from suburban neighborhoods and somewhat well-off parents.

My first year at Heritage, when I was about ten years old, was also the first year the camp offered an inclusion program for kids with higher-functioning forms of autism. At ten, I still embodied some of the staples of Asperger's: specific areas of interest, repetitive behavior, and difficulty with speech. For instance, I knew more than my fair share about tigers and Batman, and was well on my way to learning all there was to know about Ninjas, Japan, and the Beach Boys. I imitated sounds and voices and at the same time had difficulty with speech. People with Asperger's also tend to be physically uncoordinated, and I was no exception there. But by far the most influential symptom of Asperger's in my life has been difficulty in social interaction. And therein was the main goal of the inclusion program: to put us in situations with "normal" kids our age, so that we might develop our social skills by observation and interaction.

This wasn't a complete inclusion; we had our own special group of helpers and aides who followed us as we joined our age group and tended to our specific needs. With our not-so-subtle shadows, we moved through our day.

Even so, many of the kids in the program kept to our small group, or even to themselves. Interaction was difficult, and most of them developed their strongest friendships with children with special needs. I had a good friend in the program who I had known since age five, and made a couple of other friends in the group besides. But despite my similarities with this group, I couldn't identify with them entirely. The majority were in their own world, and content there, playing Game Boys, Pokémon, self-invented role-playing games, or just talking.

Out of the inclusion kids, I was the highest functioning. I took advantage of the opportunity to interact with the "normals" and tried desperately to make friends with them. Audrey was one of the few friends I made. I started to hang out with her and a couple of her friends on the playground or at lunch, and at once realized how bold they were. That was all it took to develop a small crush on her. Audrey and her friend Darryl would recite the "Uncle Fucker" song from *South Park*, for example, and found it hilarious. I remember finding it funny, but not in the same way, as I still saw no need to use curse words. In another memorable conversation, she teased me for not knowing the meaning of the word "dildo." When Darryl left, I still hung out with Audrey for a while, until one day when she told me blatantly that I wasn't as much fun as Darryl. Seeing no way to remedy that at the time, and it being close to the end of summer, our friendship faded. "I had a huge crush on Darryl back then," she had told me at the video store. "I know you did," I replied. It's clear to me now that she had been attracted to Darryl's boldness. Being in a world of social structure that was still alien to me at ten or eleven years old, I don't think I had it in me to be so bold then.

The more I tried to befriend the normals, the more I shunned my autistic peers. I am sure some of them recognized that they were looked down upon and misunderstood by the other kids, but I don't know how much they cared. That was the difference; I cared a lot. Whether or not my fellow inclusion kids noticed that their involuntary mannerisms or noises drew the normals' laughter, I certainly did. I certainly wouldn't be the one to be ridiculed for having a tantrum when my mashed potatoes touched the peas.

I went with my group to play dodge ball, soccer, basketball, and several other sports I didn't excel at. Dodge ball was my favorite, but I don't know why. I was terrible at it. My lack of coordination limited my catching and throwing ability severely, but at the start of each game I would give handling the ball a try. After failing at that, I would stick mainly to the dodging aspect of the game, taunting those on the opposing team and throwing myself to the ground or jumping as high as I could to avoid the ball. When I got hit, which more often than not was early in the game, I would start pouting. I remember loudly growling in frustration several times. I think some part of me knew that by throwing a tantrum I would just be drawing more attention to myself, but I was far from caring. All I understood was that I had failed where others were succeeding and I couldn't stand it. I wanted more than anything to be good at sports, just some kid who didn't have to have an aide come to calm him down after he lost. The fact that I couldn't succeed set me apart in my mind's eye. This was the standard I set for myself.

Eventually, people took notice. Another normal I met and befriended noticed my struggles with dodge ball and took time to help me out. "Hold it like this," he'd demonstrate. He'd watch as I attempted, and if I did something wrong he told me. Later that day I got my first out in dodge ball when the ball I threw knocked the ball out of an opposing teammate's hand. We hung out a few times and had some interesting conversations about whether or not wizards existed. But he was no Audrey, and I don't remember his name.

The day of the camp's own Olympic Games, someone else stepped in on the behalf of the inclusion kids. Appropriately, the Olympics consisted entirely of athletics. Also appropriately, the inclusion kids were suffering. Before one of the last races, one of the head counselors took all of the present normals aside for a huddle. I, along with the other couple of inclusion kids, was excluded. I could tell something must be going on, but my mind was focused too much on the competition to care. The counselor assembled the whole group, lined us up, and then made some short, odd speech about pacing ourselves. The race started, and almost immediately I could tell something wasn't right. I was giving my all, as I usually did, and to my surprise I began passing people. I kicked it up a notch, and was flabbergasted when I moved to the head of the pack. My confusion was such that as I passed the two front-runners I called out:

"Guys, what are you doing?"

"Pacing ourselves," they breathed.

I crossed the finish line in first, and was swarmed with congratulations. It should have felt great to win. One honest win would mean I could forget about all of those defeated dodge ball games, all of that anger. But the fact was, it wasn't honest. The fact was, I had put two and two together before I had even crossed the finish line, and I wasn't happy about it at all. I understood that the staff had good intentions, and mentally I thanked them for thinking of me. But I wasn't stupid. The thrown race meant nothing to me, and I wanted a rematch. One I would lose. Because it wasn't about the race or the win at all. It was about fitting in. I was dissatisfied with and even embarrassed by my autistic friends, so I looked to the normals for acceptance. The race meant they had found me out. It meant I was labeled and had to face an inherent challenge of living in two worlds: having to make the most of defying classification. I worried that it meant that whichever group I chose, I wouldn't feel fully at home.

PART 2

MIDDLE SCHOOL

CHAPTER 9

BIG CHANGES

For twenty minutes or so at the end of our workshops, Mom and I open up the floor. By then, we've both said our piece; we've related some semblance of the story of our struggle in the hope that it resonates with the people sitting in the audience. But because autism exists on a spectrum and because no two cases are the same, we feel that we can't have done our jobs completely if we don't answer some of the specific questions that are on people's minds.

The questions range from typical to completely unexpected. Sometimes people just want to say thank you, and sometimes they want THE answer to their struggles. Do I still have trouble with food textures? (Yes.) What was it that got me interested in making friends? How has autism affected my romantic and sex life? Mom and I pass the mic back and forth depending on if it is a parenting or personal experience question.

As you can imagine, we have some frequently asked questions. One of them is: "How do I get my son/daughter to be more comfortable with changes in routine?" How can a parent make it so that it isn't the end of the world when summer turns back over into the school year, when we move, if there is a substitute teacher?

It's a tough one. No denying that. I still get pissed off on a daily basis when my household appliances don't work the way they're supposed to. What do you *mean* the button on the remote is busted? How am I supposed to use a drawer that, if I didn't know better, I'd swear was *trying* not to work correctly? I get angry because the reality is at odds with my expectations. This situation causes stress for anyone, but for an autistic person, the change of routine can be a death sentence.

The answer that we give, more or less, is that the change must become part of the routine. I usually give an example from my own life because, hey, it's what I do.

When it came time for me to enter the big bad world of middle school, those around me foresaw that I was going to need some extra help. By the time I was done with fifth grade, I had already been to the middle school. My mom and I went again at least twice. The more familiar I was with the place, the more comfortable I would be, and the less alien it would feel. Even though I was a smart kid, there was no way I was just going to show up the first day and figure things out like everyone else.

It took some doing, but Mom met the special ed. crew at the middle school and got my schedule ahead of time. We went into the school again, my third time being there, and walked my schedule room to room. I was even allowed to go and meet some of my new teachers, including my new aide, Mr. Noel. Now I was skeptical about having a one-on-one aide. Coming straight from elementary school, where I enjoyed the relative anonymity of a classroom aide whom no one knew was there for me, I was worried people would think there was something wrong with me. But when we went up to that fourth-floor classroom, I asked, rather bluntly, "Who's going to be my aide?"

Everyone laughed—the tall, burly social studies teacher, my mom, and someone who looked rather administrative. I saw Mr. Noel sitting there, smiling. I couldn't be angry. He spoke in a French-Haitian accent that was at first indecipherable but fascinating.

"I am! Nice to meet you Dylan, we going to be good friends." "Those" sounded like "doze." "Friends" had a mysterious _w_ in it where the _r_ should have been. I could feel my mind opening up to the possibility that this might not be such a bad relationship.

SCUFFLE

Something about this building seems wrong to me. Part of this I will later be able to attribute to the general sense of things not being right when I go through transitions. On the up side, the building is bigger, cleaner, and more organized (the stairwells are labeled with big green arrows pointing up or down—this will always remind me of a highway). But the sixth grade is all the way up on the third floor, which is really the third floor when you consider the basement. I walk by the lockers, which change from green to yellow to blue as Mom and I make our way up the correct stairwell, and I get a flash of panic about my new school. Each kid has a locker. If all of the kids have to use their lockers at the same time, how will anyone be able to move? How many kids must there be? Will I have to learn a new locker location and combination every year that I am here? What if I never see my friends from Wilson again, and what if I have trouble making friends? What if I just never learn to find my way around this place?

My legs are tired when we reach the top and I am left to wonder why the kids with the smaller legs are supposed to walk up all of these stairs to get to their first class.

I feel the familiar weight in my stomach as I chug up the stone steps from the cafeteria to the blacktop. As usual, I have wolfed down breakfast in near record time so that I will be able to play at least half an hour of schoolyard football before going into class. Maybe some of the bigger eighth graders will be out today so that I'll have a challenge. I'm never the fastest kid out playing, but I'm often one of the biggest. I enjoy counting the one-down, two-down, three-down, up to seven and then rushing the quarterback. Tyrique is a big kid two years older than me and he has been showing me the ropes a bit. When he knocked me over I learned I can never block someone with my back. As two of the biggest kids, we usually end up on the opposite teams trying to block each other from getting to the quarterback. My progress up the stairs is slow and I wonder if I should have had that second pop tart.

When I get to the top, the football kids are already playing. I start to jog over and their game slows down. As the play slows down and the kid returning the ball for the other team starts to become surrounded, I can pick out Angelo. Too late, I notice that he is standing up far too straight and is about to get whacked.

Sure enough, Darnell lowers his shoulder and sends Angelo flying onto his back. A crowd gathers as Darnell stands over Angelo taunting him.

"Woo! What the fuck is up, huh?"

Everyone is laughing or standing around while Darnell goes on, unmoving. My steps become faster as I pass those wasting their morning socializing under the basketball hoops. Ignoring Darnell, I push my way in and lift Angelo to his feet.

"You alright?"

"Yeah, I'm fine!" Angelo is pissed, but he isn't really hurt and doesn't want any part of Darnell's nonsense. Before I can say anything else, Darnell is in my face.

"Bitch," he declares. I'm a bitch because I helped my friend up? A knot tightens in my stomach. He's not backing down. I don't like confrontation, but my anger is winning the battle.

"I know *you* are," I tell him, using a strategy taken directly from arguments with my sister. The surrounding crowd lets out a collective "ohh." As I could have expected, this infuriates him even more.

"I ought to whoop your ass right now," his voice cracks and he gets even closer to me before turning and walking away. I look over at Angelo, who is still adjusting his glasses. Oh no, he doesn't get away with it that easily. My stomach is a bag of coals.

"Yeah, that's why you're walking away," I scream, and start walking away myself.

"That's why I'm what? That's why I'm *what?*" Darnell shouts. I continue walking away. I've succeeded in making him angry, but I think that's all I want. If it's one thing my short months of Karate training have taught me, it's to avoid a fight.

Suddenly, I'm pushed from behind. I stumble, but I don't fall over and I keep walking. I won't get dragged down that easily, and I won't get pulled into a petty fight.

Seconds later I hear a *thunk* and Darnell's fist slams into my jaw from behind. In my new rage I take a fast step to try and catch him. But after a smile and a look back, he has run off and disappeared into the crowd.

What am I to do? If I run after him, I won't catch him and I run the risk of looking even more stupid. Why did I walk away in the first place rather than face him? Am I going to get into trouble for this? I can't just back down from people like that, but I hate confrontation and fighting so much that picking a fight never seems worth it.

In the midst of these jumbled thoughts stands one that I come back to more and more lately. What are the other kids going to think? Before I know it, there are tears streaming down my face. Did I really deserve this embarrassment, just for making sure my friend is alright? Do I look like the biggest fool, or what?

"Oh my god, you're so *cuuute*! What happened?" A couple of older girls see me crying and come up to me. I don't know whether I feel flattered or humiliated. They are cute, themselves. Trying desperately to man up and wipe the tears away, I explain what happened.

"Why don't you go kick his ass?"

"Well, I do know Karate..."

"That's it, go fuck him up!"

I stammer and walk away. Even years from now, my anger will reduce my articulation skills to exasperated sighs as I feel helpless to step outside of my angry loop of thoughts to explain to anyone how I feel. My jaw doesn't even hurt that much, but I can tell it will bruise. I can't find a way to explain to them that I'll never catch Darnell, and if I do, and I hit him back, the lunch monitor is sure to catch me and blame me for the whole thing. I don't want to get into trouble for something as stupid as this, but I sure as hell don't have to let this kid off of the hook.

I walk into Mrs. Anders' class. The Troy Aikman bobble-head doll and the teacher's thick New York City accent don't clash in my mind yet. I won't notice Oliver, Nina, Chenoa, or Ebony this morning, but set my books on the table in front of my chair and go up to Mr. Noel.

At about five foot five, Mr. Noel isn't much taller than my mother. His golden chain and the face of his watch glint against his caramel-colored skin as he sips his coffee.

"Mr. Noel, Darnell just punched me. It doesn't really hurt or anything, but…"

"Where?"

I sigh and show him my jaw.

"Who did that? Darnell? Alright, we gonna go see Ms. Zasha." Having grown up in France and Haiti, Mr. Noel's accent is thick and I am still getting used to it. His face is more stern than usual as he leads me into the hallway. Usually, he jokes around with the kids and his laughter and smile will be among the most genuine I'll encounter. But right now he's all business.

"Dylan, tell me what happened," Ms. Zasha urges. She has called both Darnell and me into the office, and we sat side by side.

"I came up to play football, and Angelo was laid out. I came to help him up, but Darnell was standing there and he called me a name."

"Okay, what did he call you?"

"He called me a bitch." For some time to come, I will feel weird using curse words around adults.

I explain the rest of the story from my point of view, and Ms. Zasha turns to Darnell.

"What's bothering you this morning? Because I don't think you woke up and said to yourself 'I'm going to hurt Dylan today.' I don't think it had much to do with Dylan."

"Actually, it had a lot to do with Dylan…" Darnell starts, but Ms. Zasha isn't having it.

"Alright, Dylan, you can go," she says. Later the same day I will give Darnell a Fruit Roll-Up to try and make friends. The elderly Irish nun who teaches religious education will agree with me when I speculate that Darnell was simply reaching out to make friends. My mom won't.

The physical pain of the injury itself is nothing. The day it happened, I rubbed my jaw, trying to loosen up muscles I imagined had tightened. Darnell never threatened me again, but had no shame about bragging to his friends and even me about punching the big kid and getting away with it.

"He walked around all day holding his jaw saying 'Darnell punched me,'" he bragged one day in the locker room.

"I think it would be a very different fight now," I mumbled, pulling my shirt on and getting out of there.

TESTING THE BOUNDARIES

Sixth grade was about the time I remember really starting to worry about my reputation. I started talking about how I knew martial arts and even gave demonstrations here or there where I would kick over my head or stop a punch an inch away from someone. Never again would I cry in front of a pair of eighth grade girls for a non-bleeding injury. Never again would I take a punch without giving one back (as long as I could avoid getting into trouble for it).

But as much as I wanted to be the tough kid, I just didn't have it in me. Trouble was a completely unattractive concept. Getting detention or a suspension represented too much of a change in routine. I never wanted to piss off teachers or administrators I liked. In short, I am too much of a thinker to be impulsive. My anger, while intense at times, always starts with a frustrated simmer and never involves harming anyone.

During a lunchtime football game in seventh grade, my conflict resolution method was put to the test again. Normally, the administrators and lunch monitors would only let us play two-hand touch football. But occasionally, when the right monitors were absent, we played what we called "wraps." Rather than touching or tackling the ball carrier, you had to wrap them up and stop them. We all liked wraps a bit better, but as a bigger kid I especially appreciated it because it meant I could use my power to my advantage. Wraps had a tendency to set some tempers flaring, though. A kid named Topher was running the ball down the open asphalt with Johnny, a notorious hothead, closing in behind. I'll never know whether Topher was lateraling the ball to Johnny because he thought he was a teammate or if he actually was aiming for the head. But regardless, the ball came back to smack Johnny right between the eyes.

"What the FUCK?" Johnny yelled, bent over and tearing up. Topher had long since left the scene, and a few of us were snickering. Perhaps I was laughing the loudest, but at any rate I made the mistake of standing all alone.

"Are you laughing at me?" Johnny asked through his hand.

"What?"

"You fucking laughing at me?!"

"No, Johnny, I…" The concept was there. The idea was in my head. But the words just weren't coming. Pretty soon, he was right in my face.

"This isn't funny," he said and cocked back his left fist. Before I knew it, he had hit me in the eye.

"I'm sorry man," I said, feeling my face as he bent over again. Oddly enough, I was calmer now and the words were coming a bit easier.

"Just don't laugh," Johnny said.

"I wasn't laughing at *you*, I was laughing at Topher. Like, how dumb can you be?" It was true. It hadn't been Johnny's pain I had found funny, but the utter lack of thought on Topher's part.

"Oh…I'm sorry then. Just don't laugh," Johnny said before he walked away.

Why didn't I kick Johnny's ass? I certainly could have countered the punch and gotten into a fight I could have won but may have lost terribly. At this point I had another year of Karate behind me, but I just didn't see the point. From my point of view, it was a clear case of misunderstanding that didn't warrant any further injury. Why should I fight Johnny if we could still be friends? Why not just shut up and play the game?

I didn't tell anyone about this event until my mom asked me about the red mark on the corner of my eye. Though I had found no reason to fight, I didn't want to try to explain my philosophy to a bunch of testosterone-filled adolescents. I also understood how little respect there was for tattle-tales, and coming off of that summer at Heritage, I very much wanted to be respected and included.

I was conscious of the fact that people would judge me by what I said and did. I wouldn't, for example, let them in on the fact that I didn't walk home from school every day in sixth grade, but rather to the same babysitter's house I had been coming to after school since fifth grade. I did take every opportunity possible to try to make a friend, turning to the kids who walked in the same direction as I did.

In order to fit in with the group of boys who walked in my direction (some of whom crossed the street with me one day out of the week to go to religious education class), I started to behave in ways I normally wouldn't.

"WHOA, there!" I heard Todd yell when he pushed James through a bush. James would get him back eventually. A big dude, I joined in on the fun one day, pushing Sam into a bush. He was laughing, dusting himself off when a van pulled over and a woman got out.

When she rounded the front bumper, I knew her immediately. My English teacher, Mrs. Matthews, was livid.

I understood what we were doing was wrong, but Sam was unhurt and laughing and the bush was still mainly intact. We stared dumbfounded and frozen by the secret and loathsome motherly frequency of her voice.

"What was that for? I don't ever want to see you guys doing something like that again. Do you know that's someone's property and you could get in a lot of trouble?"

I looked directly at her, my thoughts themselves frozen as I quite literally didn't know what to do. My grandmother used to tell me to "for gosh sakes, smile, Dylan," as my face dropped to the expression a mathematician might wear if the fate of the world depended on the problem he was working on. I was still trying to sort out in my stagnant mind what was happening, how we had come to be ridiculed, when she spoke up.

"Dylan, don't give me that look!"

"Sorry," I replied, an almost automatic reaction borne from plenty of scoldings for bickering with Laura, whispering in church, forgetting a very important load of laundry. I almost always face a minor freeze or brief mental shut-down when a parent or teacher scolds me.

This didn't mark the last bush I pushed someone through or the last time a walk home would end in confrontation. In retrospect, I probably didn't have to try nearly as hard as I did to gain recognition as a typical sixth grade boy.

"RUN HOME"

"You use 'yo' too much when you're starting a rap. Use different words, like 'dag, check,'" I tell Jack. Like me, he's into making his own rhymes. We've been bouncing ideas off of each other, debating which rappers are cool and which ones are wack. We don't always agree.

"Okay, I could do that," Jack says. We cross the weird, five-pointed intersection onto the street that will bring me to Mrs. Giles' house. Jack keeps talking, but I've been drifting a bit, looking at the trash by the curb and remembering the bags of responsibility that still lay on my back porch.

"What do you rap about?" he asks me. I have to think for a minute.

"I write rhymes...about whatever I guess. I have one about Tic Tacs."

"You ever cuss in your raps, or rap about more gangster shit?"

"Sometimes," I lie, "but I don't really see the need to swear a lot. And I'm not interested in drinking or doing drugs."

Jack stops for only a moment, shakes his head, and smiles.

"I can already tell you're gonna smoke hella weed and drink, you just don't know it yet."

I am sure he's wrong. I am fresh out of the DARE (Drug Abuse Resistance Education) program and still know where my complimentary shirt and ruler are. He continues to question me down the street.

"So, what, are you going to even drive?"

"Yeah, I'm gonna drive! Not now...but I will. I'm not afraid of that."

"At least you'll be able to rap about cars. What about fighting? Do you know how to fight?"

I hesitate for only a second or two.

"Yeah, I've never been in a real fight but I take Karate, so I know how."

He stops again, and so do I when I realize he's not moving.

"Really? So what would you do in a fight?"

I feel a rush I only get when showcasing something I know I'm good at. I get the same rush playing a song I know well on piano or reading a poem.

"You want me to show you?"

"Yeah."

Without any further notice, I turn and demonstrate one of the first offensive combinations I learned. I punch once towards the solar plexus, pivot, and punch towards the face with my other hand. I come within an inch or two of hitting him, but I don't touch him. The martial art I take is taught as non-contact, and one earns points by finding an opening and striking within inches of it. Those we spar with we refer to as our partners rather than our opponents.

"What the hell, are you fucking with me?"

Jack bends over and picks up a ceiling fan lying in a pile of garbage, hurling it my way. I step out of the way just in time. It hits the sidewalk with a crash as the light on the bottom shatters. Jack's eyebrows are turned down and his face is red. Though I have no idea what has just happened or how I have gotten myself into this, I start to jog away.

"Yeah, run home, bitch," he calls after me.

I walk into Mrs. Gill's house and force my literal brain not to correct Jack, that actually, this wasn't the way home. I am happy that Jack doesn't know that at twelve, I still have a babysitter. Upon questioning a year or two later, Jack will apologize to me, saying, "Hey man, you're a big kid. I was afraid you were going to do something." Though it troubles me to have been assaulted by someone I thought I was becoming friends with, I have always been quick to forgive, especially since I don't have the best situational awareness and often give people the wrong impressions. I will also derive a certain pleasure from knowing I can be intimidating. Jack and I will later be weightlifting buddies, the two most out of shape on the summer conditioning squad and with the most to prove.

CHAPTER 10

THE EMBARRASSMENT TEST

Though I have always been conscious of needing to work through obstacles and take on the things that stress me out, I have in some way always resented not being perfect already. Despite all of the words of warning from my fifth grade teachers, academics still came easily to me in middle school. Rather than serving to give me a boost of confidence, my tendency to succeed gave me an almost obsessive drive to get a hundred percent credit on every assignment I turned in. Similarly, I in no way wanted to realize that I was having trouble fitting in with my peers. It was as if I had decided that the second I walked through the doors still embroidered "West Junior High," my classmates, including the girls, would cease to be a mystery to me. As you can imagine, it didn't quite turn out that way. I was so worried about my reputation and about achieving, that without realizing it, I did and said things that would have lasting effects on how people saw me.

NOT IN FRONT OF MY FRIENDS!

It's an otherwise slow Saturday when Laura's friends Sarah and Liz come to the door. I'm up in my room when I hear Sarah (the dog) and Cocoa begin to bark uncontrollably. The action figure dressed as a Native American drops his assault rifle and in trying to pick it up, I knock over the toy truck filled with all of his foes. This will take minutes to rebuild, and all because a couple of dumb dogs can't keep their mouths shut long enough to realize that they're friends at the door.

"Alright, girls! Kennel up! Come on, kennel up!" Mom is shouting. I am hearing all of this from behind my closed door. The dogs keep barking, Sarah with her rapid, high-pitched alarm of a bark and Cocoa with her low, sporadic woofs. Several agonizing seconds pass before Mom realizes she will need to drag the dogs into their carrier. The doorbell rings again, and whether Sarah's bark has set it off or whoever is at the door is ringing again, the noise is an unnecessary contribution to the racket.

"Oh hi!" is repeated a million times and in various high pitches as Laura and Mom greet Sarah, Liz, and their mom.

My exasperated sigh deepens into an animalistic growl I am suddenly glad no one else heard. My action figures lay sprawled in anatomically impossible heaps with a plastic gun sticking out here or there. I have known Laura was having friends over today, but I am still upset at having been interrupted. Rather than bashing action figures together as I'd seen other kids do and as I had perhaps done as a younger kid, they simply stand in for the characters I imagine in my head. Most of the action actually takes place in my mind as I plan elaborate heists, chases, and getaways usually inspired by *Walker, Texas Ranger* or the Batman cartoon. I'll soon be through with action figures when I decide I'm too old for them and that they can no longer do the work required by my fantasies.

"Dylan!" I hear Mom call. The noise filtering up the stairway abates for a minute and she calls again before I can answer.

"What?"

"Dylan!" In one swift but clumsy motion, I stand up and kick over the rest of my action figures. Stomping over to my door, I swing it open and repeat my response. I despise repeating myself.

"Don't say 'what.' We say 'excuse me.'"

I can feel my eyes rolling without my help and I set my jaw.

"Come down and say hi, we have company."

Well, duh, I think as I can hear awkward giggling down below.

"'Kay." I reply, taking a moment to try to forget my frustration. It always seems like Mom makes it a point to reprimand us when there's company, and always in that cheery tone of voice she must know we hate. Some part of me knows I will be glad for these manners in the future, but being angry feels too good and is tempting. I try to let myself be calmer with every step down, but my feet want to stomp and my body twitches with frustration at the knees and shoulders. Sarah looks a lot like her mother—blonde and with glasses. Liz, her fraternal twin, has brown hair but also wears glasses. The moms have moved from the foyer into the living room and after I say my hellos, the girls move into the basement. Most people probably wouldn't be able to tell from first glance that they were twins, but to me, their tone of voice gives it away. They both have the same sweet, high-pitched voice with the relaxed cadence. In the carrier, Cocoa has plopped herself down with a grumble, her head between her front paws, and looks depressed. Still standing, Sarah-the-dog gazes out from between the bars with those deep, sad-serene eyes that never quite left the puppy stage. Laura and I have made up human voices so that we can narrate dialogue for them in funny situations. I imagine canine-Sarah asking me in her nasal, defeated whine: "Hey, what did I do? Look, Cocoa never gives me any room. You've gotta get me out of here."

Sarah and Liz's mom has left, and I'm making my way to the kitchen for some leftover pizza when Mom asks me to put the laundry over like I said I would this morning. I think twice about asking her to release the dogs, and descend the stairs to the basement.

"I don't wanna be here," I narrate for Cocoa in the lower-pitched but charismatic voice I've assigned her. A sudden urge for flight takes hold of me and I dash down the rest of the stairs, screeching like a pterodactyl as loudly as I can.

"Dylan!" I hear from above.

"Be quiet, you must," I imitate in my Yoda voice as I pass the playroom.

When I've put the laundry over and started the dryer, I stop outside the door a minute to listen and give a Chewbacca call before I head upstairs.

Later, when they've left, Laura takes me aside in the dining room.

"Dylan, I know you get excited but you can't make noises like that in front of my friends!"

"Why not? It wasn't directed at *them*," I retort. I don't like being made aware of my faux pas especially by my little sister. I am nowhere near the stage where I can appreciate her for keeping me honest.

"I don't care, it's em*barr*assing!"

"Kay, sorry," I say before walking off. It isn't the last time I'll embarrass myself or my sister in front of her friends, and it won't be until I begin to review scenarios in my mind that I'll feel some latent embarrassment at my own actions.

EMBARRASSMENT'S UNEXPECTED GIFTS

No one likes to be embarrassed. But the more I think of it, I realize I must be thankful for all of the times I felt that pang in my stomach, all of the times I felt that cold blood of regret. I have known several other autistic individuals who don't seem to have the awareness to even feel embarrassed. They bring their hands above their heads or put them down their pants, making noises to themselves, and the far-off look in their eyes tells me that they're far from caring what other people think until a teacher tells them to quit it. Even then, they rarely turn around with red cheeks, checking to see who noticed. The embarrassments taught me valuable lessons and gave me plenty to look back at and laugh about.

Recently, I sat down with a group of my friends who I've known since middle school. Laughing, we recounted stories of the early days.

"You remember when we sat next to each other in social studies?"

I smiled, knowing what was coming.

"We'd get our quizzes back and I'd have, like, a fifty-six. But I'd look over at Dylan, and Mr. Noel would be there trying to calm him down."

"Damn it!" I mock-shout, slamming my hands down on an imaginary desk and joining in the retelling.

"And Dylan would have, like, a ninety-five and be twice as upset as I was!" Todd finishes, and I'm there laughing with the rest of them. Mr. Noel did a lot of calming me down. We took a lot of tense walks around the hallway, and left a lot of math problems unfinished while my temper settled.

But it wasn't until reading class one day, when we got tests back, that I really realized I had to start calming down. Attempting to boast politely about my success, I told those around me that I had gotten a ninety-eight.

"Are you mad?" Annette asked me. Perhaps for the first time, I recognized the blatant sarcasm in her voice.

"No, of course not," I responded, attempting to cover for all of the times I had probably flipped out in front of her and her hot friends.

I CAN'T "SPIT"

Middle school is awkward for everyone, but it's even more awkward when you realize *you're* the awkward kid, when you realize your music choices and ambitions might not gain the acceptance you were hoping for...

All around me, chairs skooch backwards and kids file in and out of doors. The lunch ladies are taking orders for sandwiches and those exiting the line try to figure out where they're sitting next. I eat like a wolf and I got to lunch early, so I'm already done, my Styrofoam tray and milk box gone. I've got my jacket on one arm when I see a group of kids sitting at their table. Victor is sitting with a few of his friends I recognize and a few I don't. They all wear their clothes even baggier than the rest of us and sport do-rags and FUBU shirts. I always forget his name, but the kid with the long, thin face and the red shirt is sitting over there, too. I take my jacket the rest of the way off and shuffle over.

"What's up?"

"Not much," Victor says through a sandwich.

"Yo, what's up? You got something new?"

I smile only slightly, and hesitate a bit and then I start. The words come easily; I spent quite some time last night memorizing them. While I'm rhyming, I notice them nodding their heads, whispering, nodding to each other.

"...cause I'm a gangster, not just a wangster, if you're under my rank you gotta call me sir, call me Hollywood, that's my name, they're like who's the son-of-a-bitch with all the girls and fame—"

"I had enough of you," one of Victor's friends says coldly and abruptly.

"Okay," is all I can think to say. Time to go play football. A cold wind flows into me while I hear the thin-faced kid say,

"Yeah, them niggas at the high school, they can spit."

My gut clenches. This same kid told me a couple of weeks ago that my raps were good. But it's true, I really can't "spit." I've only ever tried to rap from the top of my head while alone in my room and came to the conclusion that it was hopeless. In college, when I take on freestyling again, I will laugh at my shame and reconsider my impossibly high standards for myself. 'Cause for a middle school kid rapping about Tic Tacs, I'm not half bad.

The Tic Tac Rap
Your breath is like thunder
and it really makes me wonder.
Whoa stop the act you need a Tic Tac.
Take one along, your breath is too strong
you been stinking so damn long.
Take one at night,
in the morning, you'll be alright.
But for right now
Poof! Be gone, 'cause your breath is too strong.

CHAPTER 11

CHORUS

Okay, so maybe it took me a little too long to realize that the rap game wasn't for me. Nevertheless, finding one's music is a huge part of coming of age. As if having to rap for my snickering grandma and aunts at family get-togethers hadn't been enough of a clue that I wasn't serious, I threw in the towel on the rap thing right after that last encounter in the cafeteria. It just so happened that among the kids I spoke to on a regular basis were a select few that steered me (I still say correctly) onto the path of metal and punk music.

I was already an autistic kid with aspirations to be a socialite but I am retroactively proud of another seeming contradiction in my life. I was a metal head who sang in chorus. Or, at least that's how I liked to think of myself, though the reality is that I was a choir kid who got into metal. I had joined chorus in the third grade, but perhaps never grasped its significance or understood how much I enjoyed it until I went to Area All-State in fifth grade. In a real performing arts center, in front of a real audience (of mostly parents), I recall having my first genuine feeling of pride that I had been a part of a project bigger than our little elementary school choir that (I thought then) had actually sounded good. I auditioned for choir upon entering middle school and only then did I truly feel I had entered the world of chorus.

Now, chorus in sixth grade was hugely different from chorus in fifth grade. To my relief, I would finally be singing tenor instead of soprano or alto. By the end of my stay in elementary school, I was getting sick of having to reach for all of my high notes.

At my first few rehearsals I realized proudly, and perhaps a bit nervously, that there really weren't too many other sixth graders in Concert Choir. The chorus classroom was attached via a divider to the music classroom, both painted intense yellow with scratchy blue carpeted risers. From my home on the back riser, I'd let my consciousness drift to the blackboard and whiteboard at the front of the room, to the black grand piano poised and begging for use, to the mysterious-bordering-on-senseless walk-in closet, and through the rows of sopranos.

Inevitably, Mrs. Howell would bounce to the piano and play some heavy-handed chords to try to break the chatty, post-lunch ruckus. She was tall, thin, and almost impossibly enthusiastic. Her blonde hair somehow stayed straight and clung around her head and neck despite her almost constant movement. She had a smile that looked to be in danger of flying off of her face and brightly lit eyes to match. After a I, IV, VII, I chord progression, she'd inform us screechily that we were about to get started, or would simply begin warm-ups.

Mr. Saul, who taught alongside her, was her complete opposite. For all of the intolerably corny jokes my dad has made in my lifetime, he may have hit the nail on the head with this pair.

"She's like a bowling pin and he's the bowling ball," he remarked after having seen them together, presumably after my first middle school concert.

If Mrs. Howell provided the energy and enthusiasm, Mr. Saul exuded an almost somber grounding presence. It may have come directly from that tired, authoritative stare. When he crossed the room towards all of us still bustling to our feet and Mrs. Howell trying to sing scales over our voices, more of us would join in singing. If he had to, he'd call specific people out, especially the wise-guys.

But he had a way of making you feel relaxed. I remember he helped me pick out and work on "They Call the Wind Maria" from *Paint Your Wagon* for an upcoming adjudication. On one night in particular, with the adjudication closing in, everything was going wrong. My pitch was sharp and my voice was strained. I couldn't stand still and I couldn't relax. What was more, with my attention now directed at my newfound anxiety, I slipped up even worse. From my unique vantage point from within that vicious cycle, I was watching my music unravel.

"Look, sit down. No, I want you to put your chair backwards, like this and just sit down, relax. This is a cowboy song. Go ahead, feel like one." Within a couple of renditions I was back. But when it came to keeping us in line, I now realize that he barely had to raise his voice.

In middle school, I was what you might call a rule follower. I remember always being that way. It could have something to do with the not-so-far-away memory of well-placed motherly wrath, but I think my tendency to stick with the rules comes from my natural desire to keep a routine. Nothing like getting into trouble to throw a wrench into a routine. Also, without a wealth of friends, it was relatively easy to keep focused on the task at hand (namely, belting "I love to sing" in an ascending scale at the top of my voice).

I did however enjoy others' mischievousness. Several of the basses in my section made it a point to change the words to the warm-ups but without Saul getting wise ("I love good sex" was a favorite substitute). This was one of Dante's favorite games. Here was a kid who was obviously a football player and who looked like he should already be in high school. He made a habit of gloating to younger students, me included, that his body was more mature than theirs. I usually let such remarks slide without comment. I mean, the dude was huge and one got the impression that he also had several huge friends. But once during a competition he called me out, saying that his big strong voice contributed the most and in fact carried the section. When we sat together and listened to the tape the judge had made, one remark made me laugh. "Oh, don't do that, basses. Don't stick out." After the song, Dante had turned to me and told me that, he guessed, he'd been wrong.

I never dreaded going to chorus at lunch. It was a fascinating place for me, and not just because I enjoyed singing. In sixth and seventh grade, I was able to sit back and observe how the older kids handled things; how the basses flirted with some of their soprano friends; how people got away with making jokes behind the teachers' backs. What's more, lunch was a time I was allowed to do things myself, without Mr. Noel. I'm not sure I would have admitted it back then, but I certainly looked up to those seventh and eighth graders who knowingly and unknowingly showed me the way. But lunch time rehearsals tended to be rushed, and when I did get bored, I found myself wishing it were tomorrow or yesterday so that I could be on the football field instead. It was during the periodic one-and-a-half hour after school rehearsals I found I did most of my learning musically and socially.

Well that, and field trips.

CRASH COURSE IN ETIQUETTE

"I sleep with my eyes open. I have very light eyelids. It freaks people out. They can't tell if I'm sleeping or if I'm awake."

The bus has just started its long journey to Boston. It's one of those busses with the nicer seats, TVs, and even a bathroom in the back, and Dad, here as a chaperone, is floating around somewhere. I've been swiveled around, talking to Les. I've heard of people sleeping with their eyes open, but I'm not sure whether or not to believe Les. Before the year is through he will have told me that he knows five martial arts, that his first knuckle was fractured to make him a better fighter, that his father knew twelve martial arts, and several other tall tales. I'm not sure if he keeps telling them to me because I respond noncommittally or as if I believe him, or if he simply enjoys lying.

Sitting next to him is Bruce, a big kid with messy hair and lazy eyelids. I had a *Revolver* rock magazine and he had a skating mag. I asked him what kind of music he listened to.

"I listen to weird music."

"Like what?" I was getting into System of a Down, Slipknot, and Blink-182.

"Like Rancid." Bruce will strike me later as a person whose sense of humor and demeanor might unfairly peg him as a stoner. Sitting behind them is Gordon, a short, red-haired kid who had brought his PlayStation with him and hooked it up to a portable screen. Earlier, he had whipped out a humongous package of AA batteries and came to my aid just as I thought I was going to have to endure the six-hour ride without any music at all.

"You never go on a road trip without a ton of batteries."

Normally six hours in a vehicle would spell hell for me. While I am on the road I fantasize about being anywhere else— in a room with video games, on a beach, in one of my favorite horror stories. But because this trip has the added label of "field trip" and because all I have to do for several hours is to eat and talk to people, I was already enjoying it.

Before I know it, maybe an hour or so into the trip, I find myself in a situation all sixth grade boys brag about, given the chance. I am mid-conversation with Molly, an eighth grader I've barely said a word to. All of a sudden, the conversation takes a bizarre turn.

"Are you from California?" she asks.

"No. Why?" Was that a serious question?

"I don't know, it seemed like you might be for some reason." She sounded disappointed. Should I have said yes? What would have happened then? Why do I have such trouble talking to girls, especially the cute ones?

As she rejoins some of her friends, I put on my headphones and start up my newly re-juiced CD player. I pop in a new Blink-182 CD and listen. I get lost amidst the frantic guitar and what even I recognize as juvenile themes. But what appeals to me most is the sarcastic sense of anger I can't quite put my finger on. I smile when I come to a specific line about female rejection so systematic and predictable, the singer is left to wonder if it's all a conspiracy, if there's really someone in charge, asking or ordering them to behave a certain way, to act intentionally against him.

I still have trouble talking to anyone except my close friends about the girls I like, so when one of the eighth grade girls asks me who the sixth grade crushes are, I stammer and flush.

"What about Kelsey? Everyone's hot for Kelsey," a girl I think is named Emily prods.

"I guess, yeah, she's pretty." It felt extremely odd to say, and judging by the response, I know it sounds that way too. But it's good talking about it so casually. The whole thing feels like a lot less of a mystery to me.

After our performance, still dressed up, cumberbunded and starving as only teenagers can be, we situated ourselves for dinner and a random, trivia-based game show. Tacky, old-school-style podiums wait in one corner of the room while we set our stuff down at our desired tables, finishing a conversation about terrible drivers.

"...probably has the driving skills of a deranged howler monkey," I joke with Les on the way to the bathroom.

"I like that," he says. "Do you mind if I use that?"

"Yeah, sure," I jabber.

"Yeah? Okay, guess I won't then."

"No, I mean yes I don't mind. But you'd have to ask Johnny Bravo, that's where I got it from."

But he's not listening and we file into the bathroom. Standing at the sink, I'm listening to another conversation at the urinals.

"No, but really, Bruce's mom's chicken just melts in your mouth," says Les.

"I don't know, this stuff looked pretty good," Aaron responds.

"I don't know, my dad's chicken—"

"Dylan, we're peeing, you're not supposed to be here!" Les suddenly cuts me off. Again, I have that cold sensation deep within me, like I've done something I can't change. I'm not doing too well at my job of being a chameleon. Every time I catch myself being awkward, I feel like I'm taking a step back. It's a step back from ever getting girls like Molly to like me. It's a step back from ever being the kid people seek approval from. It's like letting myself down. I dry my hands and shake it off.

Later, the trivia-based game show is drawing to an end. My team—with Aaron, Les, Sam, and Bruce—is in a tie with another team. The announcer, in his best cheesy-gameshow-director voice, is telling us we must improvise a performance in order to decide the winner. For some reason or another, we had named our team "Milk."

"It can be a cheer, a song, a dance, a rap," the host went on. At once, all eyes fell on me.

"Dude, Dylan, you got this," yells Sam.

"Yeah, just go up there and rap," prods Les.

"I...uh...I'm not sure."

"Come on, man, we've heard you, you're good!"

"But I can't freestyle!"

Now I regret showing off my rhymes on the bus. Les takes center stage and we win the competition anyway.

CHAPTER 12

HEAVY METAL
KEEPS ME SANE

I'm free, sliding into the cool morning. The air, cooler than I thought but still refreshing, washes a wave of goose pimples over my arms. The Blink-182 shirt I'm wearing seems suddenly thin. I pat my backpack down, checking for a football and some binders. I've taken to catching breakfast at home or on my way out the door so that I can spend the entire morning playing ball. Before leaving, the kitchen clock read 7:37. Right on schedule.

The walk to school from my house takes only seven minutes if I'm walking full speed. Today, I have System of a Down on my side. I'd like to think it makes me walk faster, but I know I'm just enjoying myself. My hair tightens to my scalp as it dries into purple spikes. Halfway up Helen Street I almost trip over my skull-pocketed pants and hike them up almost all of the way. The quiet residential bustle of people getting ready filters its way in between songs. In a strange sort of way, it all seems to go with the music. My steps and heartbeat in time with the drums, the dotting of kids on distant blacktop run to the pace of the guitar solo. Serj screaming sounds exactly how I feel—intense, anticipatory, somehow chaotic. I have always been recognized as loquacious and extroverted, but when I'm on my own, my mind fills up the space around me. I am somewhere lost between a daydream attempting to predict today and an intense focus on internalizing the music. I am on the blacktop rushing the quarterback and wrapping him up; I return a kickoff sprinting and weaving my way untouched into the end zone while Serj screams about changing the forests into sand.

Dropping my CD player into the bag, I grope around for the football and watch the slow-pecking geese wander the fenced-in

West Middle practice fields. Upon moving to Binghamton's West Side, we had started taking Sarah and Cocoa here to run around with a few other dogs and their owners. They've since banned dogs for obvious reasons, but I have fond memories of my fat canines chasing geese in vain upon their arrival. One day when I can take a break from Karate, I'll join the football team and crash my way to the starting squad here. But until then, I live on the other side of this fence.

On my way across the street, I see a pigskin already flying and replace my own. Six or seven of the regulars have arrived before me, and every second they waste playing catch is valuable game time. The morning bell rings too early no matter what. I'm about to try to fulfill my regular duty of herding the others into a huddle so we can start when I see Todd coming through the gap between fences.

I point to him with my chin and ask what's up. He shakes his head and smiles, looking me up and down.

"Why the hell are you dressed like that, Dylan?"

"Why the hell not?" I'm not unprepared for such a reaction.

"Smart kids aren't supposed to wear skull pants and spike bracelets and dye their hair purple."

"I guess this one does."

Still laughing, he waves and heads in. His bangs stand up straight in the front just like everyone else's, just like I do mine up some days. Something keeps me from dressing up in band shirts and bracelets every day, but I'm unsure what. The fact that I go directly from school to religious ed on Tuesday certainly has something to do with it. Tomorrow, I'll probably be wearing polo shirt, jeans, and my new Timberland boots. Either way, the music in my CD player will be something that rocks. As long as I don't understand it, I don't expect anyone else to; just accept it.

"Who's captain?" I shout, running over to put my backpack on the line that separates the football field portion of the blacktop from the basketball hoops.

A WORK IN PROGRESS

Third period finds me in my social studies classroom which also happens to be my homeroom. In seventh grade, we have to take an integrated math and English class, and the English portion takes place here. Ms. Belle has been replaced with a fairly lax substitute today, and since most of us have finished our work, a substantial bustle permeates the room.

Nina is sitting next to me, drawing something. I hadn't noticed, but she's damn good. Her current doodle is of a punk-looking teen with the letters AWIP on his pencil-shirt. Upon closer inspection, the A is actually the anarchy symbol.

"Hey, what's AWIP mean?"

She giggles and her dark eyes light up.

"It's a band my brother and I started. Er, are starting. It's A Work in Progress."

I glanced at her sideways for a moment before I realized.

"A Work in Progress is a work in progress?"

"Yeah!" she laughed again, and looked rather cute, her shoulder-length soft black hair falling on her Misfits shirt.

"How'd you come up with that?" I glanced at the substitute, who had turned her chubby, uninterested face partially into a magazine, and back to my friend.

"Well, the other night I was talking to my brother, Pedro, about the band. Neither of us had come up with a particularly good name for a punk band, and I asked him what he had decided on if anything. He told me 'Our band's name is a work in progress.'" In a tone of voice that suggested a detective who had just solved a particularly perplexing crime, she added, "Our band's name is A Work in Progress!"

"Sweet!" It's a good name for a band. Catchy and recognizable as a facet of our everyday communication, yet unexpected and begging a deeper analysis.

This is a cool idea and quite an opportunity. I'm not known for being subtle, but that's really okay.

"Do you guys need a singer? I don't play an instrument. Well, not really. Well, I can play some piano, too, but you might not need that in a punk band. I've been in chorus since third grade, but I've always wanted to do something…cool with singing, know what I mean?"

"Okay, let's hear you," she says, tilting her head and squinting slightly.

"Well, uh, what should I sing?"

"Anything, just go for it."

Not the answer I'm looking for. It's disarming as hell. My brain's frozen, the cursor held fast by an hourglass.

I'm supposed to sing? In class? This feels like sixth grade religious ed when the old Irish nun asked Kelsey and me to sing something from the upcoming chorus recital. Except here there are more cute girls who may or may not already think I'm a weirdo. Here, there are popular kids who could spread word of my possibly terrible singing faster than a forest fire. But what am I, someone who dresses in black and reads Stephen King but is afraid to put myself out there a bit?

I chose a Good Charlotte punk ballad about not being the rich guy in a dating scene supposedly full of materialistic women.

It went well, and I didn't miss a note. Nina was nodding and smiling. So why are Adam and Matt laughing? Angry, I turn around.

"What?"

More laughing. Matt puts his head down on the desk.

"What? Why is it funny?"

And how can I hope to be in a band if I were to just get on stage and have others laughing at me? They shake their heads and give noncommittal answers. Whether it's in my imagination or not, I feel more eyes on me. Even the circle of preppy girls in the back corner seem to smirk at me peripherally.

"Good, you sounded good." She's smiling, but I don't think it's sarcastic. Why is it I don't seem to like Nina? We like kind of the same music, though I like more metal. She's short, and I'm tall, but who cares about that? If I wanted to, I could see myself asking her out. But no, it's the overly done-up, preppy girls who catch my eye—the ones who wear too-tight, expensive jeans, travel in sneering packs, and date Aéropostale types; the girls who listen to MTV music and leer at me for being upset with a ninety on a test; the ones I can only fantasize about approaching and with whom I have little to no common ground. It feels so futile, and I've barely even tried. What's the point of existing on the fringe of acceptance? Wouldn't it be easier to just give it up and find acceptance on the fringe? Such are the innumerable *joys* of straddling social dimensions.

THE POLITE PUNK

"So, what makes you punk? What's the last punk thing you've done?"

"Well, I…"

Am pretty much a rule follower? Didn't realize this audition had so many requirements?

"You there?"

"Yeah. Well, I pretty much hate the preppy kids. And…and I love messing with people, like in the mall and stuff. I went up to one lady on a Tuesday, told her, 'Please tell me it's Friday,' and she says—"

"Dylan!"

Crap, I forgot Mom was cooking fish. Don't come upstairs. Don't come upstairs.

"I went away screaming 'oh no, the aliens! Haha?'"

"Uh huh. That's cool. So what bands do you like?"

"Dylan, dinner! Is that you on the phone?"

"Hmm…Good Charlotte, Blink-182, Rancid. Hey can you hold on for a sec?"

"Sure."

I'm a punk alright. A punk who answers his mother politely and lies about doing punk-like things. Thank God I thought to leave my phone in my room.

"Whaaaat?" She's standing at the bottom of the stairs with her arms on her hips.

"Dinner, honey. Who's that on the phone?"

And here's how it's going to happen. I'm going to be out here politely explaining to my mom at length who I'm on the phone with and why I want to join a punk band, and Pedro's going to hang up on me.

I explain to my very curious mom—who only knows me to call Cal, Angelo, or Franky—what I'm doing, and am surprised to find Pedro still on the line when I shut my door again. I ask Pedro if I can call him back. I won't.

Sarah and Cocoa are sharking around the center island tilting their noses upwards while Laura and I load up our plates with rice and lemon fish.

"Who was that on the phone?" Laura asks at the table.

I sigh out loud, and Mom gives me a look. The thought of repeating myself stresses me out, but I'd better get used to it.

"It was my friend Nina's brother. They're starting a punk band called A Work in Progress and I might be their singer."

"Oh, really? That's awesome, Dylan!" Laura has always had my back.

Mom says: "A punk band? Maybe you can wear your Flock of Seagulls hair-do. I think it would work out perfectly!"

I keep eating.

She ignores my eye-roll. Even though she's being good natured about it, I know I will at some point have to have a talk with her and convince her that being in a punk band is safe and moderately socially acceptable.

Under the table, Cocoa sighs. Unlike Sarah, who sits transfixed by the meal, Cocoa just wants to be with us while we eat.

METAL AS A CATALYST FOR ACCEPTANCE

The first time my mom caught me listening to heavy metal, she couldn't believe it. *The Scorpion King* DVD I had gotten for some holiday or other included Godsmack's "I Stand Alone" music video. I had it on repeat several times before I got sick of it.

"You can't really like that music, can you? It's just noise and people shouting. It's not like they're singing or anything."

"It's more about the music," I returned. This was my only solid argument, but I didn't quite expect her to understand, just like I hadn't when a classmate introduced me to Slipknot.

"I like the music, but they're just shouting, I wish they'd sing."

"It's more about the music," Drew told me. He kept his hair spiked up and wore goth-looking pants and black shirts. Our resource room teacher, was desperately trying to get him to focus on the task at hand. So it was an acquired taste. Every food except blueberry muffins and liverwurst is an acquired taste to me.

I tried to use every minute of heavy music to work in me, transform me into someone better, edgier, unafraid to stand out. Yes, it was finally starting to dawn on me that I stood out, and not always in a good way. My brand of humor commanded me to commit small, eyebrow-raising acts of social suicide such as screaming, "I'll eat you alive!" in the middle of Spanish class (to be fair, it was a line from a Limp Bizkit song). I had yet to understand a crucial bit of humor, of writing, of human experience: other people crave context. That my mind had made some vague connection between what was happening in conversation and that song lyric wasn't enough for my classmates.

"Look out, he'll eat you alive," Pete warned the rest of the class.

Their conversations obeyed train tracks. Mine went off-road. While my wild and layered connections helped me to write meaningful poems, they didn't always help me make friends.

If I wasn't going to be able to blend in that well, why not get comfortable standing out? I could turn heads and be proud of it. I was pretty sure this is what Pedro meant about doing "punk things." I ate up Good Charlotte and Blink-182 lyrics and found more and more that I was the kid in all songs who couldn't fit in, didn't understand girls, and resented the preppy kids who ate up all the female attention and played sports effortlessly. On the days I had to trade my football time for chorus at lunch, I started sitting and eating with Sam, Jeff, Danielle, and Gordon, kids who all listened to punk and metal. At their table, strange topics were not off limits. We could talk about how dumb most people were, how the popular kids like Aaron threatened to take away a slice of our identity by wearing band shirts. We conjured up narrow but hilarious scenarios in which the popular, pretty girls came in wearing black and sporting cloth bracelets, rock pins glinting on their backpacks. Unlike Les, who had once told me I only fit in with the eighth graders because I was tall, this group seemed to actually enjoy my company. Sam, who always wore Blink shirts and talked with Jeff about underground rap turned me on to Rage Against the Machine, Dead Kennedys, Rammstein, and several others. When he asked me "what's up?" he waited for an answer. I *could* be the smart kid who dressed in black and spiked his hair, and if people didn't understand, well that was kind of the point, wasn't it? With a little help, I had stumbled upon a mindset, a haven, a niche where having the tendency for unprovoked references and bizarre timing so characteristic of the nearly indescribable inner workings of my world wouldn't work against me. This setting provided an escape from the pursuit of acceptance without relinquishing power. I had my ear re-pierced and with some difficulty forced another stud through the original hole I'd had made in third grade. Two silver hoops with black tribal designs hung in one ear, matching my grey-flamed skull shirt. I bragged about going to Good Charlotte and Godsmack concerts, generally leaving out of my account the detail that my mom or dad had taken me.

CHAPTER 13

THE TROUBLE WITH GIRLS

But my newfound strategy wasn't to be a way of life; there were holes. I couldn't talk to Clarissa or Molly or Kelsey about heavy metal if I wanted to get close to them. Most girls weren't like Nina or like Raven, the short, spunky punk from chorus and eighth grade homeroom. Most of the time I didn't know what to say to the girls I wanted to approach and so I didn't approach them unless I was encouraged.

"Yo, come on man, we gonna sit next to the girls today," Franky pushed. He's seen me eating alone as I sometimes did before choir and came hulking over.

"I don't know man," I managed through half of a sloppy joe. I gazed over. Kat and Anna and basically half of the good-looking seventh graders poked at their lunches and gossiped.

"Tell me you don't wanna talk to those girls, son, I *know* you do." He had me there. After all, what did we talk about on the nights that he and Cal slept over?

"Gotta Make. Shit. Happen!" Franky stomped in emphasis of each word, nearly losing his chocolate milk on the last one. I couldn't help but laugh.

"Alright," I stood up. Franky was right. What the hell else was I doing? If I ever wanted to learn how to talk to girls, I'd have to start sometime, right? Franky, having lost his virginity halfway through seventh grade, was a prime candidate to try and show me the ropes a bit. I gathered my things and approached the girls' table as if through pudding.

"What's up ladies?" Franky asked, extra velvet in his voice. I smiled and we slid in. Some sat meekly, others chatted amongst themselves, and some did talk to us. Franky was trying his game on Anna.

"So, whatchu usually do at lunch?"

I laughed awkwardly to myself, not contributing much to the conversation. I mean, I answered and asked some small-talk questions, but nothing much. Before long, I had to leave and go to chorus. I excused myself rather quickly, making my way past the pool and the water fountains. What the hell, I had time for a quick drink.

I was halfway up the stairs when Franky shuffled down the hall, calling my name.

"Yo, Dylan, come here!"

"Yo."

"Check it out. Not the dark-skinned girl…"

"Anna?"

"Yeah. Not her but her friend… She said she thinks you're cute."

"What? Who? Kat?" He had to be joking.

"Yeah, her! She said not to say nothin' 'cause she has a boyfriend—"

"But she called me cute?" I hadn't noticed any indication of interest whatsoever at lunch.

"Yeah, you should come back and chill!"

I turned back up the stairs. No way I'd be on time if I went back; I might already be late.

"I'd love to, but I have to go."

"Ah, damn Dylan, you're killin' me! Skip it just this one time!"

"I'm going, man. But tell me if she says anything else!"

Letting a hand flop down dramatically, Franky smirked and turned around.

What could I believe? I plodded up the stairs, wondering: if Franky was indeed telling the truth, why was I still heading upstairs?

I ROLL THE DICE...

Maybe I could get further going after girls I knew a bit better and came into contact with more often. Clarissa was a likely candidate, or so I thought. She hadn't known me during the turmoil of my elementary school years; we always ended up in the same religious education classes; her long brown hair and gorgeous body attempted to steal my attention whenever we happened to be in the same room.

But things had been complicated with her from the beginning. In sixth grade her group of friends started to question me like chickens pecking:

"Dylan, are you single? We know this eighth grade girl who likes you."

"Dylan, do you like Clarissa? Do you want to go out with her?"

"Uh, why? Who's asking?" I'd finally answer.

"Clarissa wanted to know."

Imagine my surprise, butterflies in my stomach beating steel tip wings into me, ears getting tomato-red, when I met her on a stairway on the way out of school and was shot down.

"So...Rachelle said you wanted to know if I liked...uh... wanted to go out with you."

"Nope," she said, just like that, matter-of-factly. "It must just be Rachelle making trouble."

Even the most socially challenged of individuals would have caught that that particular conversation was over.

But the mixed messages didn't stop there. At the end of science one day, Clarissa dropped a folded-up piece of paper on my desk and walked stiffly out of the room before I could respond. In a few years' time, I would have understood that she hadn't meant anyone else to see. I unfolded the paper as quickly as if it might have contained gold. It did—her phone number. She needed help understanding the "King Phillip Came Over from Germany Saturday" (kingdom, phylum, class, order, genus, species). Could it be that she was interested? The mnemonic device seemed awfully straightforward to me. Science homework wasn't a reason girls gave guys their phone number. But on the phone later, the conversation deadened.

"Yeah, so that's all it means, it's how life is classified."

"Oh, thank you."

The beat of silence extended almost forever, and we said our hasty good-byes. That was when things began to get really weird.

...AND COME UP WITH SNAKE-EYES

"Alright, let's see, when is your birthday, November, right?" Mr. Noel sat behind me, today's paper draped over the sides of the desk. His brown eyes sparkled with mischief as he read my horoscope. His vowels took on the French *r* coloring I had somehow come to associate with his kindness, a warmth that had followed him here from his homeland and which he couldn't help but share. Some of my classmates were put off by his joking manner, and that upset him to the core.

"Oh, and there is a love interest, Dylan! I think it must be Clarissa!"

Instantly, my ears turned hot. Was my crush that obvious?

"Well, maybe, er... How do you know?"

"I just notice some things (tings) when you two are around each other (udder)."

My brief-flaring hope would be extinguished later that day, when, passing Clarissa in the hall, I once again tested her.

"Hey, what's up?"

She stopped, shifted her books impatiently, giving me a look. Not the one I was hoping for.

"Could you, like, stop asking me what's up every time you see me? It's kind of annoying."

That settled it. I would keep my head high, but I wouldn't give her another look. Horoscopes were bullshit anyway. This is the last bit of attention or hope I'm giving her, I thought.

THOU SHALT NOT LOOK

"Look down my shirt one more time and I'll kick you in the balls!" Clarissa whispers from across the table.

"But I wasn't... You know what? Whatever."

I'm trapped in the basement of a convent classroom decorated with optimistic page-sized posters ("God, why don't you send people to find the cure for AIDS and cancer? *I did, but you aborted them all*") across from a hot, angry eighth grader in a low-cut shirt. Mrs. Thomas, the religious ed teacher, is explaining the Ten Commandments and I am beginning to think this is an argument already lost. In my peripheral, Todd laughs silently, mouth open wide enough to catch a fish, and rocks back and forth in his chair. I hope he falls out in front of God, Mrs. Thomas, and everybody. I hope his still-growing legs betray him the same way he betrayed me not a half-hour ago.

The few of us left dawdle in dead halls. The one or two teachers left pace idly like lions before mealtime. Student-made graphs, posters, "art," and stains decorate the walls. Several lockers to my left, Clarissa fumbles with her lock. Some kid's hyena laugh spills around the corner, and then there is Todd's. I shake my head, trying to concentrate.

The end of any given day finds me standing at my locker, scrutinizing my books and binders. My agenda and my backpack stand open on the floor. Because Mr. Noel helped me organize, my books and binders rest in two neat rows, locker shelving unit repaired and put to use rather than broken, hanging, in the way. Because I generally refuse to put homework assignments into my agenda, I must rely entirely on memory. My Spanish binder is the last to stuff into my bag. Papers spill out like icing; apparently, Mr. Noel hadn't gotten to that one.

"Cut it out, *Todddd*," Todd mocks Clarissa and they both giggle before I slam my locker shut (for effect) and Todd leans on the locker next to mine. I bend to pick up my backpack and he tries to push me, but not hard enough. I pretend to stare at his old, white Nikes before I fall into him.

"What's up Todd?"

"'Sup, Dylan?"

Todd's usually-silent companion, Tim, isn't around so today it will just be the three of us crossing the street to church. We each sneak a couple of glances at Clarissa, who is still crouched down, picking up books.

"Alright, Dylan, looks like we'll have to go ahead because *some people* take too long." Clarissa giggles sarcastically behind us and we move on. When we're almost at the staircase and completely out of earshot, Todd turns to me.

"Oh, man, I love looking down Clarissa's shirt."

I laugh quickly, guiltily.

"Well, don't you?" he prods.

"Ha, yeah, sure."

Clarissa catches up.

"Hey, Clarissa, Dylan says he likes to look down your shirt!"

"Ugh! He can't get a girlfriend, so he has to stare at me!"

I glance seething hate into Todd, knowing full well the expanse of years in front of me, and the quick, enduring, virus-like growth of rumors.

THE DANCE TEST

The sunset bleeds rust orange into the school gymnasium. Growing pockets of overdressed sixth and seventh grade boys with wood-stiff hair watch the doors for the slow trickle of girls. Next time, I will get here later. I've already made my rounds through the dark halls and to the bathroom, and now finally some of my friends are showing up. Some pop song I've made it a point not to know is pumping bass directly into my ears and Mr. Adams, a speech teacher turned DJ, stands behind his console bobbing his head too earnestly. Wearing too-baggy sweats and a huge smile, Franky lumbers through the doorway. We do our half-minute-long handshake and stand back as the gym darkens and tries to be a dance floor. Thankfully, the music isn't so loud we can't talk.

"Yo, so is your girlfriend coming?" I have a way of masking the jealousy in my voice.

"Darien?"

"Yeah." How many girlfriends does this kid have?

"Nah, me and her broke up. I realized we was only staying together cause the fuckin' was good. I'm about to dance with mad honeys tonight."

"I still can't believe you lost your virginity." I shake my head and sweep the room. How many of these others are ahead of me already? The eighth graders have started to arrive, including some girls I know from chorus but not well enough to approach.

"I'm tellin' you, son, after you do it, it just makes you want more. I can never look at a girl the same way again, just thinking about…"

He trails off, and I see why. A small flash of girls in revealing, colored dresses enter the auditorium and circle up almost immediately. A fourteen-year-old boy has *eight times* the amount of testosterone in his system than a grown man, my eighth grade English teacher will tell us. I see Clarissa almost immediately. My eyes scroll over her and linger on Rachelle, who's wearing a dress tighter than I've ever seen.

"DAMN." The word still has the juicy tang of forbidden fruit. It tastes orange, like Clarissa's strapless dress.

We flip through them from afar like the shoebox full of loose pages of old *Playboy* magazines Franky brought over the last time he stayed the night. Girls make me forget all about self-awareness and social propriety. I forget entirely that Franky and I, the biggest kids in the gym (including the eighth graders), are standing alone on our own personal island of gym floor.

A caramel-skinned girl with curly black hair approaches us and my stomach yo-yos.

"Rachelle wants to know if you're going to ask her to dance or just stand there and look?"

"Yeah, yeah, we were 'bout to," Franky says before I can even think of a response.

The clock says a whole hour has passed, and the gym has since gotten packed. In the hallway, some of the more awkward guys have given up on dancing in favor of chasing each other around. In the middle of the floor, the girls I've deemed unattainable dance expertly with each other or against the popular guys. Kelsey, every sixth grade guy's crush from last year, is among them, dancing with Brian. She has braces like me, but hers actually make her look cuter. How do these Abercrombie-wearing kids get where I want to be? Is it really that easy for them? My own green polo, though name brand, looks suddenly dull. Swaying bodies. Rap and pop music I borderline hate. The night is slipping through my fingers and I've yet to get a dance.

But yet, there's hope. Earlier, I asked Clarissa to dance and to my surprise she and three of her other friends moved towards me. Oh lord, what had I done? This wasn't a slow song. They swung their hips and danced seductively closer for a full twenty seconds before I realized I hadn't the slightest clue as to what I was doing. I stopped all stiff attempts at motion and yelled over the music that I didn't know how to do this, that I'd return for a slow song.

"Kat will dance with you...for half a song."

Now, with Kat across from me, "Beautiful" by Christina Aguilera comes on. You're supposed to look girls in the eye. But not too much. Her hips are smaller and sharper than I thought, like my fingers might meet each other around her back. Whatever hesitation is keeping Clarissa and Rachelle back is missing in her, or she left it back in the girl-huddle. It's pity sex at a G-rated level but I haven't earned the luxury of caring. I know what they all say about me.

"Look, Kelsey thinks you're stalking her," Tran will tell me in eighth grade. Kelsey, who will be in my classes until senior year of high school, will quicken her pace whenever she walks past me, and zip up her hoodie all the way if she even sees me looking at her. Between the business with her and Clarissa and my non-sequitur outbursts during, it seemed, every crucial moment, my reputation was pretty much cooked. But it wouldn't end there.

"We used to watch you in chorus, checking out the sopranos. Your name was an answer to several of their profile quizzes for AOL Instant Messenger—an answer to the question 'Who stalks me?'" Ben, the pianist, will be sure to enlighten me two years late as we're starting high school.

I have an ability to hide my shame somewhat, to let it roll off of me. But it sticks to me like one of those hellish burdocks seeds, pricking me stiffly even years later. How can I have been so ignorant to think that my fascination for the world of blossoming women went unnoticed on my face from day to day? Most days, I swing back and forth with myself. If I don't at least try, I'll never get anywhere talking to girls. But when I can't even be in the same room with them without getting into trouble, giving up is rather tempting. "Always finish what you start," a mantra Master Sterling tells us towards the end of particularly rigorous kicking drills, usually gets the final word.

I'll file away this air Kat has about her, this boldness laced with calm, a girl with a certain edge. At least I'll be able to say I got a dance.

CHAPTER 14

DOCTOR B

Even though middle school has been pretty ugly for me at times, I'm not the only one who struggles. Towards the back of Doctor Bartholomew's English class, Angelo has his eyes narrowed at Mr. Martin, who looks like he might be your uncle, your father's younger brother (the one that drives a pick-up and listens to Slayer).

"I don't care, just leave me alone!" Angelo's tone is stormy with a seventy percent chance of losing it.

Mr. Martin throws up his hands and, swiveling back around to Bartholomew, I wait for shit to hit fans.

Dr. B looks up from his podium with a Jon Stewart-esque smirk. He dresses in shirts and ties and has hair that at any time borders on wild fro. I once heard him say he could bench-press three hundred pounds, and come to think of it, I'm sure he can. His voice has the thunder of a Coliseum announcer but thankfully I have never once heard him yell to get us quiet.

"Angelo, I predict you're going to marry out of prison."

Angelo's eyes press up against his flexed eyebrows and look down towards his paper. He mutters that it isn't funny while everyone enjoys a good laugh. But his scowl isn't set in stone; I can see the corners of his mouth twitching towards a smile.

DR. B CALLS ME OUT

I felt sorry for the guy in the way only someone who's been there can. English was always the obvious choice for my favorite class and I considered it my home turf. In the mean hallways of 8B, in math class, in gym class and school dances, I sometimes felt like I'd been given the controller to my own life having only skimmed through the tutorial. But English was easy, and because it was easy it was fun. So, as revenge to the kids who had bested me in sports or in front of girls, English class was where I tended to show off. At the end of a test one day, Mr. B encouraged those of us done early to write a poem on the back of the paper. I wrote an elaborate, lyrical, and borderline sexual ode to a chicken. Dr. B struggled over my handwriting, but people laughed. He read Ken's poem, which was intimidatingly full of images and sharp language, and said that it was "really something." I had accepted defeat, but I'd do it my way. "Mine was, too," I said aloud, realizing too late that I hadn't quite mastered the use of irony or sarcasm in conversations.

"No, your poem was silly. This is serious, and it's good."

Okay, I'd had my ass handed to me. I'd shut up now. But the gauntlet had been thrown. I'd known right then what he wanted from me. The competition wasn't with Ken—there was enough room for both of us, so to speak. The competition was with Bartholomew's expectations. And I fully intended to blow them out of the water.

DR. B ON THE MERITS OF TELLING THE TRUTH

Dr. B's class was easily my favorite of the day. He had us read Vonnegut's "Report on the Barnhouse Effect" and "EPICAC," wasn't afraid to teach us Shakespeare, and had interesting stories to tell. He even took the whole "telling the truth is easier than lying" maxim and made it funny.

"We used to have this house on our block that was empty, and you know we'd go fool around in there. I had told my parents that I was going to the library or bowling or something but instead found myself there at that house. It got dark and we put the lights on, not thinking that, duh, there were no blinds. Anyway, we got caught so we snuck out the back and ran and someone called 'David Bartholomew, I see you!' I mean, of course she did. Look at me, I'd look like a freakin' cue ball running down the street. So, my dad clearly found out that I hadn't been studying."

He bobbed his head and his mass of tight curly hair shook, making it look even bigger than it was. I could imagine him running down the sidewalk, taking up half of it even as a kid. He clearly lifted weights, and though he dressed professorly, Dr. B looked like he might be able to throw a couch. Maybe that was why he could control the class without yelling. He's the only teacher I've had before or since with that capability. If we started talking out of turn, he'd simply stand there and after a few seconds everyone would just inexplicably get quiet. The most I ever heard him say was "Excuse me."

OUT-CALM

Mr. Martin took longer than any student I've had sign my yearbook, and even longer than the teacher or two I handed it to. Patience was still more a goal of mine than an attribute, and I could feel my legs twitching. He was about as big as I'll grow up to be, but for then I had to look up to him to speak. As he handed me the yearbook and then shook my hand, he said something like this.

"Dylan, it's been a pleasure. You've got a head on your shoulders so just out-calm and use it. And don't worry, you're not going to hell." I remember him smiling when he said it.

I would have called myself a fairly devout Catholic back then, and Mr. Martin, a metal head and atheist, was far from it. I couldn't understand when he explained to me why it was I couldn't scare him when I jumped at him from around a corner; why, unlike for me, fear of death and the miracle of cheating it didn't make life anymore divine.

"Listen, man, I've had more brushes with death than I could tell ya. There was this one time my brother and I were surfing and the waves caught us in a bad spot. See, the tide kept taking us and crashed us down onto this sharp pile of rocks. So we'd climb and almost reach the top before another wave would come take us and slam us down again. I've survived that, and I've survived multiple falls from the top of houses."

"But didn't that make you think? About God, about *why* you're still alive?"

"Hey, I used to be Catholic. I did the whole altar boy gig and everything. I lost faith when I saw an uncle of mine doing exorcisms in Florida. Some of these people, man, they were really possessed. You could just see it. But a lot of it was bullshit. And then, well, I started getting into Iron Maiden and Slayer." He smiled, but he still looked solid as a stone. He didn't make a shred of sense to me.

He knew my world was stretched between my Catholic faith, my developing logical brain, metal music, and, of course, girls. Having just read Dante's *Inferno*, I was writing some pretty doomed-sounding poems and one of them, which Martin must have gotten his hands on, was about hell. His comment about hell was what grabbed me then but the idea of out-calm would really stick with me later. *You're a smart guy, but you get so frustrated with yourself,* he wrote. Frustration was a good thing. It kept me dissatisfied with my status quo and allowed for improvement. It was a very palpable emotion in a murky internal sea. But maybe my anger could use a break. Maybe I could use a break. Maybe everyone around me, who had to hear about it whenever my routine, plan, or grades got botched, could use a break.

It embarrasses me to think on that moment in eighth grade. Of course I wasn't going to hell; it may have taken his saying it, but I fully understood it and now felt foolish for being afraid. Embarrassment could quickly lead to anger directed at the fool inside, the one who had failed me.

"How do you think that other part of you [read: the fool] feels when you get upset?" a therapist once asked me.

When I feel embarrassment, I have an opportunity to learn something, and the sooner I can turn those red cheeks into laughter, the sooner I turn the ego back to working *for* me, the sooner the lesson can take hold. I had already come so far from the kid who couldn't handle being thrown a curve ball (literally or in the form of a pop quiz), the kid who could hardly look a girl in the eye and ask her to dance. But it's almost like the very hormones cruising through my veins at that age prevented me from putting things in perspective. There was only the embarrassment and the redemption. Many long, guilty years were to pass before I could realize the true value in my fun mistakes.

Chapter 15

TAKE-AWAYS

It was the end of eighth grade, and we had no material to learn or tests to take. Just a few days' worth of class periods left (we could count them using hands and toes now). We toted around our yearbooks, and our teachers desperately tried to find stuff for us to do. In Spanish class, we did little more than wait for the bell. A few of the girls including Alicia wore white shirts branded (in Sharpie) L.O.G. for Lady of a Gangster. As they stood at the board writing down lists of nicknames, I wondered how I ever could have lusted after someone whose values were clearly so different than mine.

My punk rock friend, Nina, had packed up and moved in the middle of the year; we still hadn't gotten the band together. But more importantly, that meant that I had no one for steady conversation, just time to wait. When I again turned my head back to the whiteboard, I was irate: "Dylan—Hillbilly Genius."

"Whoa, buddy, don't erase that!"

"Yeah, well don't call me names then."

I was back in my seat and silent before any argument could ensue. How could I have gone so wrong? Was it that time in math class when she had overheard me saying to a fellow goth-dressing dude that I hated rap? Or another time I professed (politely) that I preferred metal to whatever was playing? Or the time after chorus I had walked down the hall with Big John and Russ, blaring Disturbed's "Down with the Sickness?"

In retrospect, I shouldn't have been *that* disappointed. Part of this whole metal/punk image was making waves, right? Well, that I had done; I had made myself an outsider and I had done it well. Only seldom did I get invited to play manhunt with the neighborhood kids. Kelsey still thought I was a creepo even though (or perhaps because) I told her outright to stop thinking I was stalking her. Most Friday nights, I ordered pizza and watched rented videos with my mom and sister.

A MEASURE OF SUCCESS

Life wasn't *all* bad.

I might not have been the social enigma I dreamt of being, but I at last had friends. It's funny, and I didn't realize until I heard my mom say it years later to a crowd of parents, but it was only at the turn of fifth or sixth grade that it dawned on me I actually wanted friends. By then, I was convinced I had grown out of the imaginary realm Laura and I went to when we hunted leprechauns or waited up for Santa or staged self-made plays for Mom. And while we still played together, I'm not sure Laura didn't take that personally. And it isn't as if Laura and I had stopped playing together (every year, even into our teens, we'd concoct elaborate schemes to somehow get our Christmas stockings out of Mom's room without waking her or the dogs). My world just needed to expand.

By eighth grade, Cal, Franky, and I were close friends. Sleep-overs, complete with pizzas, pro-wrestling video games, and porno mags were becoming a regular thing. At my house, we let the dogs chase us around the yard, and we played Nintendo until Mom heard me cursing and made me (to Franky's delight) take a break. We prank-called people. When we could get a ride, we sat in the back of the movie theater and made our own commentary complete with sex jokes and fart sounds. To say that we told lewd stories would be a vast understatement. I liked these dudes and I owed a lot to them.

I could trust them to keep my secrets and I could trust them to somehow lead me to mischief. They made me feel like I was doing something right in all of this gaseous, violent boyhood, as if I had overthought or put too much stock in the distinction between my inner world, to which only those closest to me had any significant knowledge, and the broader, more or less connected, functional, social network.

But eighth grade was also when I started hanging out with Angelo. Sure, I had gone to a birthday party of his (the first time I ate an entire pizza), and he sat near me in a bunch of my classes. But something about the kid still irked me. He was confrontational: there were rumors (most of them true) about him biting other classmates into the sixth grade, and he routinely got into arguments and refused to back down. He still insisted that he had once been saved from a lightning storm by, as he put it, "a bunch of cows and chickens" that crowded around him. But beyond that, he didn't seem to care at all what people thought of him, and his state of mind fascinated and disturbed me. While I at least pretended to keep my wild and woolly side under wraps, Angelo went through the first half of high school shouting at random people that he'd devour their souls. Even though we spoke a lot, even though I found him hilarious, I tried not to be associated with Angelo.

When I stopped trying to sit next to and make conversation with Kelsey in homeroom, I started sitting next to Raven. I knew her as the short, cute, gothic chick from chorus, but one of the first times I sat next to her, something dawned on me.

"Do you remember that time in sixth grade when I asked you to slow dance?"

"Oh my god! That was so awkward, we just, like, stood there and I wouldn't slow dance with you because I was dating Chris."

"I almost didn't recognize you. You had braces then and Eminem was plastered all over your locker."

It turned out Raven and I had quite a bit to talk about, even besides music. I had found someone to unload my poems on. The darker, the more image and emotion heavy, the more she liked them. It didn't take long for me to wish she wasn't now dating Caleb. But a nice little surprise awaited me when she signed my yearbook. At the end of what had to be one of the longest entries I'd ever seen in a yearbook sat a phone number.

"First time for everything," I remember thinking.

PART 3

HIGH SCHOOL

CHAPTER 16

GODZILLA

While the transition to middle school had been mostly unnerving (well, horrifying), the dawn of high school represented for me a chance to shed some of the burden of being a semi-outcast. The halls teemed with new faces and if I could only lose my aide, I might also be able to tidy up my reputation. And my inspiration was all around me. My locker (which I immediately decorated with as many bikini babes as I could get my paws on) was right next to a couple of seniors, and at eighteen they seemed so full of the wisdom garnered within these walls that it actually changed how they looked. Their attitude was a bizarre, knowing combination of concentration and abandon. They got done what they could and fled the red-brick prison as soon as their duties were carried out to a sufficient capacity.

Sarah, the senior with the locker right next to mine, wore a lot of black like me but the comparison ended there. Whereas I felt sufficiently harried by the more rigorous social and academic demands of my new domain, Sarah was actually busy. She had the beginnings of a real life going. On top of her high school curriculum, Sarah went to trade school for cosmetics. I knew the worst was still ahead for me academically, but I still had my challenges (my still-blossoming patience and fine motor skills meant that I could barely label and color in a map in Global History). Sarah had a serious boyfriend; I had Mr. Noel and a reputation for being a creep.

Mr. Noel still had to stand over me and guide me through breathing exercises when my locker shelf collapsed and my precariously organized books and binders fell to the floor. Though I always had a peripheral hope that Sarah (or any other attractive girl) wouldn't be around for one of my stress tantrums, I still lacked the awareness to short-circuit my anger in order to save face. I had to admit it: when I saw Mr. Noel strolling up to me in the morning (at this point, several inches shorter than I remembered him) smelling of juicy fruit, coffee, and whatever cologne he wore, I was glad to see him. He knew by this point to trail behind me in the hallways and leave a vast gulf of desks between us in class, but whenever we were together, droves of other students attempted to make sense of us as they hurried by. So did I. Floating beside us as we walked in the semi-reflective surfaces of the red and blue lockers, this ghostly smear of reflection blended us together. Everything about me was expanding; I grew taller and fatter and my hair puffed out. I had the scattered makings of a beard. I was outgrowing the need for Mr. Noel, but not quickly enough. Once when we passed a cute upperclassman in a stairwell, Mr. Noel greeted her on the fly more suavely and effortlessly than I could have had I the entire morning to prepare. The light from the window caught her face for a second and coming upon us, flashed a knowing smile.

"Beautiful day, isn't it?"

"Oh, gorgeous!"

Mr. Noel saw me looking after her and grinned.

"See how easy dat was?"

The lace of her skirt flittered as she passed, and with her went all of the wonder about my future. She probably had a boyfriend with a car. She had probably voted. If she had stopped to think, she would have known exactly what I thought of her.

"Oh, sure." We had reached the top floor and the rapid, muted Spanish of upper-level language classes leaked out through the wooden doors. Millisecond-long glances through narrow windows afforded me glimpses of appropriately bored seniors in crisp, white and red football jerseys, and the collective sighs and hair tosses of everyone surrounded them. I got one of those palpable, iron-tasting sensations walking alongside all of those closed classrooms and cool hallway tiles. I thought of bookends. The seniors and I were on opposite ends of a library's worth of tests, trials, and molding experiences. I couldn't quite be sure that I would ever be looking back on it from a stage or in a prom tux, the same way a seed (if it had a mind) would ever be able to imagine being a tree. If I could have, I would have kept climbing right on up out of 2004.

A MOMENT OF TRUTH

It's the beginning of October. Flyers in the halls that pester anyone of voting age to get out and make a difference, or forever hold their peace, tantalize me with the idea of agency. Some days are better than others, but now that Mr. Noel has taken a position as a security monitor, I'm caught in a nebulous space between life eras, and what's more, I'm fully aware of it. In my first class of the day my new aide, Mrs. Bradley, sits pensively at the back of the room. I cringe as she asks me so many questions, just as my usual tablemates Ben, Dave, and Flora drift in.

"You did the homework?"

"Yup, it's all here."

"Okay. Now you know we have a substitute today. Do you want me to take notes?"

"Um…sure. I'm gonna go sit down."

She's nice enough, but she seems offended by the pictures on my locker and there's no easy comradery between us. It's weird seeing Mr. Noel around the school. He's a monitor, and that seems to suit his boundless, restless personality much better than following me around.

We do indeed have a sub: Mr. Guerta, who with his slicked hair and shark smile seems almost artificially enthusiastic about being in this strange, sterile green room to break us into groups, send us back to our tables like black islands, and guide us through the lab.

I rush back to the usual table so that anyone thinking of stealing my seat will be foiled. The others arrive more slowly and put down their books and sit carefully, the way one might settle into wet concrete. This is the toughest task of class. As with Mrs. Bradley, the relationship between us is touch and go. Usually I would be able to get them to laugh by impersonating Matt Damon's developmentally impaired character in *Team America: World Police*, or by showing off print-offs from whichever oddball prank site I'm frequenting. I have such a list today, and I pull it out almost as soon as they sit down.

"These are all things we can do to confuse people in school; take a look, man."

Ben quotes from the paper: "'Ride a horse to class, pull your paper from the saddle bag, shoot the horse away in front of the whole class, sit down, and refuse to explain anything.' This is weird, dude."

There is his uneasy laugh, but Flora and Dave flip through the rest of their papers as if they hadn't heard. Serj, a huge, sixteen-year-old Russian kid, comes in late and walks past us. Ben shrugs and nods his head towards me, and Serj returns the gesture, waving one of his huge mitts. Moments like these, I feel as though I'm on the brink of a realization. Guerta addresses us from behind the podium, shifting his weight back and forth as if he knows he's interrupting something more important.

"Today, you're going to work on a classification key. Now Ms. Wilzinski said she's explained it to you and all of the materials are on the back table, okay?"

Glancing to the back of the room, the aquarium and its huge, green-gray sucker fish stare back. The fish's name is Godzilla and for some reason all of the cool kids seem to despise him. The teacher either doesn't know or care that they make fun of her for caring so much about it, and it's become somewhat of a symbol of their mutual uncoolness. Dave catches me looking and seemingly reads my train of thoughts, a common and currently unexplainable occurrence between me and the people I surround myself with. One day, a girlfriend will explain to me when I tease about my fictional wealth of secrets, that I in fact have none.

"Dylan, is today going to be the day?"

"Yeah, how about it?"

Ben stares directly at me.

"It would be hilarious, but it's not like no one's going to see?"

Flora laughs a sputtering retort.

"Come on now, Dylan, killing Godzilla was sort of your idea, don't be a wimp."

Flora is attractive, and if she can read minds as well as everyone else seems to be able to, she already knows how I feel, how much of an extra bite her words have. It's no longer clear to me who suggested we dump powdered soap into the aquarium, or what the act of rebellion would accomplish if not to satisfy a deep, playful malevolence.

"It's not like no one will see."

Everyone rolls their eyes.

"Come on, what's the worst that could happen?"

"Oh, like it's not going to be obvious at all? Why don't you go do it, Ben?"

Mrs. Bradley taps at a crossword. Guerta paces around in between student questions, occasionally disappearing back into the staff hallway connecting the science rooms. My tablemates stare at me intently.

"I'm not doing it, not with all of these people. What, I'm just going to nonchalantly pick up that carton of soap powder—"

"What's nonchalant?"

"Don't worry about it, Flora." But Ben seems absent, following something just over my shoulder. He has the look I imagine hunters get when a set of antlers begins to distinguish itself from all of the surrounding branches. When he stands, I realize he's been waiting for Guerta to leave. He moves towards a side table with purpose, picking up the white carton and pursing its lips so that it looms open over a paper towel. Just finish it now, damn it. As far as I can tell, no one is watching. But he dumps a mound of soap so that it rests neat as a dune on the landscape of the towel. He takes his seat and looks at me triumphantly.

"Now all you have to do is pour it in," Dave chides.

Everyone at my table has the predatory stare of a chess player making a winning move. Their pressure is too great, and they know it. I'm subconsciously aware that downright weird as Angelo is, he'd never make me do something like this. Eat a lick full of the soap himself, maybe, but this, definitely not. Things are supposed to make more sense in high school, not less. Maybe the willingness to jump out on a limb and thoughtlessly do things was what separated the cool kids from the rest of us, for whom upward mobility required the work put into learning an instrument, with the chances of success commanded by the Mega Millions. If I had to prove myself, this might be the way to do it. My legs start moving before I'm entirely sure what I'm doing. Guerta is still gone and Bradley looks at that crossword a bit too intently. I stalk over to the paper towel with the unmistakable itch of eyes following me. The pregnant towel teeters in my twitching hands inches above the water and little granules are filtering out. Godzilla's mouth, open as if in constant shock, watches me like an eye from the other side of his giant glass pane. His companion, the orange-striped fish, died a few weeks ago and now he's in here with only the anchor sculptures and clay to keep him company. No. This is bullshit.

"Hey! Not cool, man. Way not cool." Guerta seems to agree. His voice comes from behind me, and I understand too late there is only one way this could have ended.

WHAT MAKES A FRIEND?

Come the end of the day, there was a group of kids I would walk home with from school. Mostly they were the group I'd walk with in middle school: Todd (who bothered me less now but of whom I was still leery), his silent and haunted-looking partner, Tim, and maybe Benny and Nate and Dave bringing up the rear. Benny was the pianist from chorus who, the first time I'd met him, had quite seriously told me that he "looked sexy and I didn't." If I was lucky, maybe Shana and Jenny would be trailing along behind somewhere.

I didn't understand then that you get to choose who your friends are. Here I was thrown in with this crowd of my cohorts from church and from the neighborhood, and the fact was that beyond all being white, middle class Binghamton West Siders, there really wasn't all that much in common between us. Shana and Jenny mingled with everyone but associated especially with the social elite. They liked the top forty. Zach, Tim, and Todd all liked classic rock. I liked progressively more intense metal like Killswitch Engage and Hatebreed.

BF Skinner and the behaviorists treated the mind not unlike a black box, a stance I sympathize with and even accept at times (despite the universe of knowledge we've developed about the brain since then). A patient's behaviors were all that were needed, and from there, you could deduce everything you needed to know. I treated the anatomy and workings of my friendships in much the same way. Friendships, I knew, were forged in the strict, senseless bonds of routine, and that walk down the mile and half of neighborhood in my mind qualified. We traveled as friends, joked and cussed like friends, made fun of each other like friends. Through the years, I've known several other people on the spectrum—from people who functioned more highly even than I did and autistic adults in sheltered workshops alike—who sincerely turned to their peers and neighbors to validate or clarify the status of their friendships.

But it's safe to say none of us really thought about any of that on our walks down Leroy Street while we haunted local pizza places, tossing the tree berries at each others' heads, forcing one another through bushes. We adhered to the implied notion not atypical of high-schoolers that whoever our friends were now were sure to stick with us for quite some time to come. Plenty of more important topics of conversation bubbled to the surface every day.

"I HEAR YOU HAVE A GIRLFRIEND"

Halfway down Leroy Street, the tightly packed frat houses and overgrown lots peppered between old, haphazardly renovated apartments halt for the consecutive traffic lights where Leroy meets Chapin and Chestnut. Between them, two one-story strip-malls—What's Your Beef? and Leroy Package Store on the even side and the Laundromat, Leroy Pizza, and Cavanaugh's on the odd side—sit as if in a faceoff all with open doors for the uncharacteristically warm April breeze.

Our pack ambles towards the doughy-slick smell of pepperoni rolls and seared steak. Todd, Tim, and Zach walk in front of me, Benny and Nate remaining an intentional distance of at least a block from us clowns, and Shana and Jenny biding their time behind them. I flip my CD player around in my jacket pocket. The Stooges, as I sometimes refer to the trio preceding me, have been snickering and cracking jokes about my girlfriend, Raven. Of course I should know better than to let everyone into my relationship at its most vulnerable phase. But I can't contain my pride. Despite the fact that I'm over a foot taller than Raven, and despite the fact that she makes it a point to dress in baggy pants and spikes, I consider having someone to call mine is one of my greatest and most improbable accomplishments. Todd is no longer the only one with a girlfriend. Maybe that's the part of this that bothers him.

At this point, I associate a rainbow of negative feelings with Todd and this group. Earlier in the year, I made the mistake of sharing with them—when the square-dancing unit in gym class came along and I still didn't have a partner—my anxiety about maybe having to dance with the disabled girls. For several straight weeks, even after Marissa and I were paired up, I had to sit back and take it whenever they decided to tell anyone within earshot that I dance with retarded girls. They continued long after I stopped trying to chase after them for saying such things. The deep and unjust echoes of such a small remark are completely lost on them, and I don't know if I should feel worse for myself or for the disabled girls themselves, who go about their days not knowing the immediate and involuntary anger I feel about being associated with them even jokingly.

And yet here I am. Todd bumps Tim, whose eyes go wide as he teeters on the curb.

"Whoa!" Todd yells and darts screeching across the street with Tim in chase, through a narrow opening in the flow of traffic. Zach shrugs, moves to give me a shove and chases after them.

"Wait for me, wait for me!" I outdo any of them in extravagance, crossing in an exaggerated hobble, yelling my refrain in a gritty voice, a cross between Chris Farley and Cookie Monster.

"Jesus, Dylan, don't scare the kids," Zach chides.

The group thins out; the four of us pick up sodas and slices with whatever change we have, and the stragglers pass us.

It's insulting to be fifteen and still be beholden to crossing guards, but we make it past both of the ancient ones on our street and their sneers. The bare branches come alive with buds like mint-green flames. The houses begin to grow and give one another progressively wider berths. Our conversation has dried up until we see Kev walking down Beethoven towards us in his khakis and buttondown. He slaps hands with all of them and then me, and beckons us to follow him in. This is a first. In the beginning of the year when they all bought some weed together for the first time, they referred to it conspicuously as San Andreas, and typically ran inside to go look at it as if I didn't know what they were talking about. When I have something they want or some way to entertain them, they're magically my friend...until, that is, they're unsure of my coolness or ability to keep a secret.

"So how's Catholic school? Those priests treating ya okay? I hear you're in chorus now, what the fuck has happened to you?"

"Why don't you shut up, Todd? I don't want to talk about it."

"Yeah, you choir-singing fag."

We crowd in his mudroom, Zach using me as a shield.

"What's good with you, Dylan? I hear you have a...girlfriend. Who is it?"

Kev's eyes sparkle and his mouth twitches.

"I think you know who it is. Raven. Laugh, go ahead, I don't care."

"No, hey, I think it's great," but he can't contain himself, and neither can Todd or Tim. Zach snickers, but I'm getting better at reading faces, and over the years his will tell me more and more clearly that I'm not the only one getting sick of the immaturity.

"Don't listen to them. It's just 'cause you're a bit of an..."

"Odd couple? You don't have to tell me. And does it look like I care?"

I stand up straighter and push my gut and chest as far out as they'll go. The attitude in the room shifts. Maybe it hasn't occurred to them that I can play jokes all my own, pretend to be much angrier than I actually am, or that I can and will do these things not simply to put them in their place but for my private enjoyment, so that in the confines of my room later that night, I can have the last laugh.

"I was just kidding, man."

"Yeah, I know. I'm out, see you guys tomorrow."

"Come play 'San Andreas' with us, Dylan," Todd calls after me.

FALLOUT

The plan to create a new me wasn't exactly working the way I'd supposed it might. Sure, I'd managed to sneak my first drink, and after final exams were over, my first smoke. But though Angelo was the one to deem the alcohol unsafe, it had scared us all. And the herb Todd and his crew loved so much, I was unimpressed with—I hadn't even felt all that relaxed or goofy; all it did was make me hungrier. I'd try it again with Franky, but due to the mega-headache his foil bowl of ditch-weed caused, I'd then swear it off till college. Okay, maybe I was too timid to party, but I'd already had a girlfriend. Only I'd gotten too clingy for Raven and so had messed that up within a week. I definitely shouldn't have told her I loved her on the third day. It had just been one of those mechanical things. When I hugged her goodbye that day, it had just slipped out. Because that's what people in relationships said to each other.

I found myself surprisingly not caring too much what others thought. It hadn't bothered me when people said it looked like I was a father walking his daughter down the hall, or they simply gave malicious smirks and gestures that, though I couldn't read them fully, I felt spelled ridicule—saying "There go the tall weirdo and the goth." I found Raven more attractive by the day. The way she looked at me sideways as if she were peeking; the way she dressed, in layers of dark. But though the physical attraction had been strong, infinitely more important was her acceptance of me, her interest in me as a (bizarre) person and a poet, the mere fact that I'd written her a letter to woo her and it had worked. So when we broke up, it wasn't social ridicule I feared, but the torture of knowing I could have done better. And to have all of that go for nothing before I'd even had a chance to kiss her killed me. The temptation was to blame my zeal on the autism. *Of course you chased her away, you dimwit. No more relationships based on stupid little notes.*

As hard as it would be to convince someone face to face that I was an ideal match, that would have to be the only option. It wouldn't be until eleventh grade that I got a chance to redeem myself and that my lessons continued.

But at least I could say that I'd had a girlfriend, and I could say I truly did have friends, even besides Cal, Franky, and Angelo, even among my teachers. It was only through the intervention of my academic support teacher and aide that I'd escaped punishment for my attempted fish murder, and even then I felt I'd escaped narrowly. Well, I hadn't exactly escaped.

When I came in to resource room the day following the incident my resource room teacher, Mrs. Francesca, came over to me with her blonde hair pulled back and her troubled brown eyes and told me the bio teacher wanted to see me. I wasn't going to be in trouble, and though Mrs. Francesca had lobbied against it, I had a small task for me to complete. My stomach was a pressure cooker of emotions. Mrs. Francesca had already done some diplomacy work with the chorus instructor to allow me to make up some private lessons I'd missed (citing, I'm sure, how my autism made it hard for me to adjust to new schedules; to tell the truth, the private lessons pulled me out of my normal classes and since I'd found it impossible to fulfill both sets of obligations at once, I'd kind of just left them alone).

After the long walk down the hall, Ms. Wilzinski made me clean Godzilla's filter. Since this was such an admittedly light sentence compared with suspension (which is probably what I would have deserved, now that I thought about it), I had a sneaking feeling that the filter wasn't why I was here. Sure enough, Ms. W sat down across from me at one of the lab tables. The immense bags under her eyes, which she said were due to her contraction of Lyme disease, gave her an intensity one couldn't help but surrender to.

"When I got the report about yesterday, I have to say I was pretty shocked."

"I'm really sorry. I had a moment back there when I realized I didn't want to do it, but, of course, that's when the sub walked in," the overwhelming urge to defend myself, to make my point of view known and thereby avoid further punishment or ridicule, was insurmountable.

"I'm glad you had that revelation, because that easily could have killed him. Dylan, I was shocked because that really didn't sound like you. If I can be frank, I don't think you'll want to hear this, but hear me out."

My gaze had been drifting away to the grout between the floor tiles. I wrenched it back and nodded.

"Those kids you've been sitting with…Ben? And Dave? From what I understand, this was mostly their idea. I know you want them to be your friends and probably think they're your friends. But I've heard what they say when you turn your back. And I've seen them move your books to different tables when you leave the room. But guess what? Guess who would have gotten in trouble had you dumped the soap in? It wouldn't have been Dave, and it sure wouldn't have been Flora. You can bet Benny wouldn't have taken the fall for you. What I'm getting at is that anyone who would try to manipulate you like that isn't really your friend. I've been letting you guys pick your own groups lately, but I think I'm going to pick them for you tomorrow and put you with a couple of the quieter kids who will appreciate your talent for biology."

I actually passed through the what-does-she-know phase of digesting criticism fairly quickly. But it was as if this new knowledge was my true punishment—to have my reality twisted around again. I had been sentenced with the lesson that (especially teenaged) people will expose weaknesses, mine being gullibility and desperation for a normal social life, without even so much as a second thought. I would have to be on constant guard, now.

CHAPTER 17

THE BIG BAD LIMAR

Getting down on myself was now more than just something that happened. And I think that my unrelenting self-criticism (an inner dialogue I still struggle with) developed as a sort of defense mechanism to drown out others' criticism with an endless stream of my own, also serving to let people know I was to be left alone. My own standards for myself would be so high as to insulate me from shame brought on by others; anyone thinking of criticizing me would have to think twice about whether or not they'd actually get anywhere with it. I have seen the same pattern among all types of people: those on the spectrum, having autistic tendencies, and in the neuro-normative. It's just that for someone who is on the spectrum and who is higher functioning, the triumph of making it past an almost insurmountable obstacle —of being able to tie a tie and iron a shirt with fingers that at times feel like useless, unfeeling wooden stumps, or of learning to be attentive of conversation but be able to crack jokes—is, well, addictive. I had started to believe what Mom and Eileen and my other therapists and teachers told me about my potential, and considering all of that, the practice of bringing every misstep up to that gleaming mountain of praise and progress seemed to me both toxic and inevitable. If I gave myself a break now, how would I ever progress? How would I ever get a license, get a girlfriend, get a car, have a date to prom, move out, and go to college? I knew people who did what was easy: higher-functioning autistic kids who still had people making homework corrections and lunches and excuses for them.

But even so, there were plenty of others who were having an even rougher time, by whose standards I was the picture of flexibility and social savvy. The kid who'd followed me around for years now, saying chicken and turkey and quoting from cartoons he knew we both watched, had found a back door into my friendship. In eighth grade, I'd gone over to his father's place to play PlayStation with two of his other friends, Zackery and Caleb. Over Tekken and some Def Jam fighting games, the four of us developed a plan to make a company that sold things on eBay. On the eighth grade trip to Hershey Park, I'd ridden next to him, both of us laughing like loons the whole way (on the ride back, Angelo ate the top of a box of Cheez-Its). In ninth grade, when I bought a bottle of rum from Ben, it was at Angelo's house where, along with Zackery, I'd had my first drink (before we decided it tasted too much like rubbing alcohol to be safe).

Up until recently, Angelo was frankly embarrassing to be around; he made it a point to act boisterously, and was volatile at times and easy to lure into feuds. While I took a more chameleonic approach, floating between friend groups and social classes and deeply regretting anything I did to worsen my social position, Angelo's attitude suggested he had no qualms about causing a scene. There were always people who clashed with Angelo and he seemed to welcome conflict, almost define himself by it. Sometimes when people asked why I hung out with him, I embarrassed myself by not having an adequate answer. How could I hurt his feelings? I'd be just as bad as Peter denying Christ. Angelo was the picture of loyalty. When Raven was starting to get sketched out by my possessiveness, it was Angelo who told me to calm it down and Angelo's advice I'd ignored. By the time I realized we had profound similarities (he had an intense love of math, computers, and video games the way I liked English class, horror stories, and movies), we already had, by my definition, the workings of a friendship. We had a shared affinity for the absurd and a tendency towards outbursts, a certain likeability coupled with eccentricity that made classmates think twice about getting close. We had routine.

THE ENERGY-DRINK OASIS

Once I walk past the brick doorway into the courtyard, Binghamton High's high walls of red brick and gleaming glass close around me like an entity, holding me closer and closer to it. The air moves through in weird currents, sometimes gathering the newly fallen leaves and dust in temperamental tornadoes. I'm still getting used to looking around and seeing not only upperclassmen but freshmen who, it's true, look really young. Laura is among these freshmen, and perhaps it isn't an accident that she doesn't really have any of my teachers. On the whole, Laura is shyer than I am. She gets out a block or two before I do when Dad drives us in because she's ashamed of Dad's old station wagon, and when I look back down Oak Street, I see her walking alone, proudly, with her long hair blowing about. And she's more prone to embarrassment. Maybe she's compensating for my lack of social awareness; I tend to feel embarrassment only when the harm has long been done.

Even now, in the courtyard, I see a group of girls, upperclassmen, maybe juniors, which causes in me twin impulses: to greet them, compliment them, somehow make reference to the football game I have this weekend without mentioning that it's JV (Junior Varsity) and I'm not starting; and to do my loudest possible witch's cackle and watch them jump out of their skin. I resist both and get ready to have my backpack inspected. For safety reasons, everyone is supposed to have mesh or clear backpacks, but since I've ruined three of these backpacks already, I have something sturdier. The pack of juniors moves on, some dangling lanyards with car keys, some giggling, swishing coffees.

Both the Oak Street and Main Street courtyards lead to this main entryway, red tile pathways lined with black mats, hall monitors, and Binghamton High's two assigned police officers, surrounding a ziggurat-like stage structure built of painted brick, white tile, and cloth benches. I usually get to school early enough to grab breakfast at the cafeteria and then climb the steps looking for Angelo. The goths and punks have claimed this structure as their morning hangout spot when they aren't sneaking outside to smoke. Some are thin and wiry, others unabashedly rotund. The oldest among them are riddled with piercings and tattoos, hair dyed a multitude of colors. Wherever they go, they are trailed by their impossibly baggy pants and dismissive, sideways glances. Angelo is up there this morning as usual, with his Game Boy.

I'm uneasy about climbing the temple of the goths. Since middle school, I've toned down my own outward expression of an allegiance to metal/rock/alternative lifestyles and ideals save for some band shirts. Not that I've stopped going to rock concerts or listening to a wider and heavier selection of music than most people I know; I've just started going to concerts on my own, and within the course of these next couple of years, I'll get to know the sacred and dangerous peace of a mosh pit. But as with my disorder, there's a certain pleasure in keeping it under wraps, in being the kid who plays football and sings in choir and wears polo shirts, but head bangs all day long. Raven is clearly more of the punk kids' school of thought which I'd abandoned in middle school (along with my bizarre love for Dante's *Inferno* and mega-dark poetry). And Angelo, well, I'd say he's also more of the type that wears his heart on his sleeve, but in reality, Angelo is something else entirely.

As soon as Angelo sees me approach, his eyebrows travel halfway up his forehead. He tilts his head back, points at me and stands up, folding the Game Boy away into his coat.

"To the Hess?" I ask, referring to the convenience store down the street.

"Never!" But he's on the way down the face of the pyramid before I am.

I point at the glass door towards Main Street and screech my best bird of prey impression. A couple of girls in Binghamton High School Swimming and Diving hoodies laugh as they make their way across the gradually-filling commons. One of these faces in the crowd is a friend of Raven's, a slightly chubby dude with slicked-back hair and a deep love for Rob Zombie.

Apparently, he has some classes with Angelo, because I can see his face lighting up.

"Warner! Get moving before I devour your soul!"

Warner turns on the afterburners and waves back over his shoulder without turning his head.

"Dude…"

"What?!" Angelo's face turns serious for a second, and he gives a look that dares me to challenge him. I throw up my hands. He never wants to hear when he's doing something ridiculous, and although it frustrates me, I know how much work it is to cram such a formidable amount of self-awareness into one moment. He'll later tell me, with the same confidentiality that I told Angelo, Cal, and Franky, that I have Asperger's, that my keeping myself in check made him realize an immediate need to calm down substantially. Awakening is rarely painless.

"So remember the girl I was talking to?"

"Kelly-Anne? That girl who's sent you pictures of at least three different people claiming to be her?"

"Yeah. Well she's pissing me off lately."

"Internet drama? I don't know why you deal with it, man." We're trying to fight a current of people washing down Main Street towards the school.

"Yeah. I know. Well here's the thing: Laurel is jealous 'cause I've all but stopped talking to her and, yeah, I know you don't understand why I go out with girls in chatrooms and message boards but, man, I wish I could tell you how different it is for me online. When I'm trying to talk face to face it just...doesn't work as well. But online, it's much easier. You know me, man. I'm a great listener. It...gives me a chance to figure out what I'm going to say. And I must say, I have a higher success rate."

I haven't thought of it that way before.

"Hey, well at least you had a girlfriend."

Angelo stops and turns to me.

"Yo. We talked about this. You had Raven, remember?"

"Yeah, for about a week."

"Well it was something, right? You have to look at it as an accomplishment."

"Do you know what happened to me yesterday? I was in Spanish class about to ask Kelsey a question, so I'm obviously looking at her, right? 'Cause I figure that what freaked her out in middle school was I always looked at her but didn't ever know what to say. Anyway, she turns over to me and zips up her sweatshirt fast as she can, 'cause she just assumes I was looking down her shirt. And they all talk."

"Dude. You gotta be more careful. I'm sneaky about it."

"But what am I supposed to do now? I have to go to Spanish. What are they gonna say?" It was going to be like appearing before a panel.

"Don't worry about it! You're overthinking things. Consider this. Imagine how I feel! Again, why do you think I go online?"

We enter the Hess and make our way to the back cooler, appropriately awed by the selection of energy drinks. It seems there are two new brands every week. By the time I take that a.m. zero period keyboarding class for the first half of my junior year, Angelo and I will have made great progress in the unofficial and thorough business of trying them all.

"What time is it?" Angelo asks after a long swig. I crack my can and pull the Motorola Razr out of my pocket.

"We have five minutes."

"You know, I gotta get me one of those." I had often made it a point to ignore fads the same way one who's never invited to tea parties reviles tea and crumpets. But God help me, this thing was cool.

"Get Cingular so that we can talk free, bro."

Binghamton High School is now the confluence of several streams of students, whose chatter begins to fill the space around us. By the time Angelo and I are back in the commons, the goths have abandoned their post, all except for a black girl with dreads and a charming smile, who everyone knows as Jesus.

"We've found Jesus!" Angelo shouts. Jesus waves in a stately fashion.

Kelsey is among the group of girls that are making their way around the corner. She risks a suspicious glance back and I catch her eyes, bright like a hare's. Angelo and I slap hands and we wander our separate ways, each of us his own energy drink time-bomb. In this moment I am not unaware of developing a habit, of carving out a moment each day that sets the course for the rest of the morning, of building a home-base within the morning chaos. I remember every cringe-worthy Angelo moment—the time we lost a badminton tournament, the arguments he'd get in with Martin and Dr. B—but it has never occurred to me that I'm not embarrassed by him, but for him. And the reason it all bothers me so much is the same reason for our inevitable friendship: Angelo is a lot like me. Without a diagnosis, he's functioning on pure intellect and survival instincts, having just as hard a time as anyone. Through the course of the next couple of years, Angelo will adjust substantially. That is to say, we both will.

GOING SOLO

All of that pent-up desire to hurry up and be something already was finally churning out fruit. By the middle of sophomore year, I'd gotten my Karate black belt along with Dad and Laura and now was helping to teach elementary school kids. I had two years of junior summer-camp counselor training behind me. I'd made Swing Choir and learned all of the choreography, albeit not without looking appropriately lost (I saw concert footage and not all of it was pretty). I'd taken part in a summer conditioning program that had nearly killed me, under a coach who routinely reminded me that I was fat or lazy or a complainer. At the beginning of sophomore year, I played offensive tackle on the JV squad and didn't start until the final game, which I had to miss because of a sprained ankle. In the spring, I'd be confirmed in the church and would never need to go to religious education again.

Then of course was the most obvious accomplishment for a sixteen-year-old, which, like my new cell phone, I clung to as symbol of both normalcy and novelty. I got my learner's permit almost immediately after my sixteenth birthday and began taking my mother and her Honda Odyssey on white-knuckle rides through the university parking lot and continued my education on my dad's thoroughly impossible station wagon.

There's something about operating a vehicle, about having to cram every bit of your awareness into the present moment, that gave a sense of awe at the agency in my life. For better or for worse, no one else has a real say in where this car is going. There is no deciding whether or not everyone's driving tactics are suitable for yourself; there's nothing except to fall into line and pay attention. What was more, I was sure I was going to be good at it. When I wasn't driving, I drank in the dream of my newfound freedom. Archetypical visions arose of Angelo and me roaring around Binghamton in a Camaro, of picking up Raven and parking with magnificent views of the Susquehanna Valley, of beating the sunrise down a highway, car packed and headed to Massachusetts or Vermont or Buffalo or wherever the hell I would find myself for college.

Halfway through high school, I had officially outgrown my need for an aide, which I thought would leave me feeling either entirely lost or liberated. But the truth was that my first classes without an aide felt about the same as they had the past four years. All of the time Mr. Noel had been shadowing me, he'd been ducking out of the room on one pretense or another—to get more coffee, run an errand, make a phone call. And even when he was around, he spent a lot of time helping the other kids in class with their answers. My academic support teacher knew that, Mr. Noel knew that, and my mom knew that. I was present at the deciding meeting with my aide, my academic support teacher, and my mom. Although Mom was on my side, she was understandably the most protective and potentially the most resistant to a change. But in the end—just as she had when it had come to changing school districts, or allowing me to go to precisely the progressively less-supervised hangouts that allowed me to experiment with drugs, alcohol, and fireworks, as I had every time I expressed interest and was rejected by girls or even potential male friends—she understood a major, self-contradictory aspect of progress: there can be none except that which springs from the motivation provided by significant risk.

But the other side to that, and my genuine feeling of the time, was that losing an aide felt like having a birthday. I was markedly older and more knowledgeable, but what did I have to show for it? Here was something I had wanted for as long as I could remember. I walked down the hall and no one followed me. I came to my locker to find it just as messy as it ever had been. Where was the real evidence of any difference or significant improvement? Only Angelo, Cal, and Franky (and a few of my sister's friends) knew I had Asperger's, which was just how I wanted it; the secret of the origin of my eccentricity was well-contained. But that meant going solo was a victory I would only be able to celebrate or appreciate in private, at least for now. I wasn't completely alone if anything were to go wrong. I had a resource room teacher, Mr. Noel, and my mother, whom I saw, as any sixteen-year-old boy would, as a last resort. But I didn't see any reason why anything had to go wrong any time soon.

THE GREAT EUROPEAN HISTORY DEBACLE

Although my school of eighteen-hundred kids, complete with our two unfortunate Binghamton City Police officers, had a deplorable drop-out rate and a reputation for breeding lunchtime shenanigans, the administrators pushed those of us in the higher education track with mongoose-like determination. Everyone took the same history class in freshman year—the level of mind-boggling easiness simply depended on the teacher. But from there, we had two options. Anyone who showed potential or any mild interest in history was urged to take Advanced Placement European History—a college-level course which attempted to cram the entirety of European history into a single school year. The rest were funneled into Global 10.

As freshmen, we had all heard the horror stories from the sophomores who had just finished taking their tests. They told us of hours spent doing something called "text notes," the impossibly difficult tests, the sheer, vast, absurd amount of material, and a whopper of a test at the end of the year. Come September, for one reason or another (nagging parents, general gullibility, freshman naiveté, displaced ambition), several classes worth of us sat down for what we hoped somehow would turn out not to be a year of hell.

A couple of days in, I would have said it wasn't too bad. My teacher and former weight-lifting coach, Mr. Limar, had delivered a fiery speech about doing hard work, not coming to class high, and earning respect. After a summer of being run ragged under the weight of support beams (literally—we had to run a perimeter of the school, three of us to a beam) and being called fat while trying to hoist weight in ways I hadn't dreamed was possible, with muscles I was just discovering, the little soliloquy designed to make good little worker bees out of us all didn't have much effect on me.

What most unsettled me was learning that we had a huge test coming up on a summer work packet that I simply hadn't received. To be fair, I should have known the class wasn't for me when I gave my interpretation of Plato's *Allegory of the Cave*. It had gone over Limar's head, so he proceeded to try to make me look dumb in front of the entire class. Similarly, even though some teacher or administrator had clearly dropped the ball on letting me in on the huge fucking packet of work that was apparently due, it quickly became my fault and my problem. I was handed a packet and good luck, the test was on Monday.

Glancing over the thing, which began with a blank map of Europe and contained an amount of reading no high school freshman should be asked to waste a summer on, my hopes of cramming were fading fast. How could I hope to get my autistic fingers to muster the strength and fine motor skill to even fill in the map? What a start to my first year without a one-on-one aide.

Even without an aide, I had help and accommodations. I told my resource room teacher and my mother, who, both horrified, sprang into action, approaching a man who at six foot ten seemed the personification of obstinacy. My resource room teacher, a kindhearted and determined Albanian woman, tried first and failed, though she spoke reasonably and logically about my state-granted accommodation for extra time on assignments. So Mom scheduled a meeting as she had done when I had to change school districts in second grade, as she had done when the special education administrators at the middle school had tried to over-regulate and micromanage my privileges and restrictions. I sat home, had dinner, watched TV, and waited, wondering about the fate of my school career. The possibility of being moved to a lower history class and in turn being relegated to a second-rate college and second-rate future bothered me no end.

THE UNEXPECTED ADVANTAGES
OF BEING DEMOTED

Mom comes home and once she's peeled the dogs off of her I ask how the meeting went. Avoiding eye contact, she produces a print-out.

"I had you moved into Global 10. And here—"

"No! Mom, I told you I didn't want that! Didn't you meet with him?" It's seventh grade all over again: I had had a less-than-brilliant math teacher, and the stress of accelerated math just didn't seem worth it, and so against my original wishes, I switched. Because of the challenges posed by my social life, I've always looked to my academic success to make up some status points, so that I could stack up better against my more popular, well-adjusted peers. I feel now as I felt then: almost immediately guilty about settling into a lower track as if I'm somehow cheating, as if the limitations imposed on me because of my disability were nothing but an excuse that I was giving up, and therefore one step farther from citizenship in the world of the normals.

"Here's why. I did meet with him, and I tried to explain your situation—that you have Asperger's, and that the state gives you accommodations including extended time on assignments. But he was incredibly rude."

From her description, I can just imagine how the meeting went. Mom, dressed nicely in slacks, shoes, a nice blouse and jacket, and carrying a thin folder, would have seemed utterly swallowed up by the school, which was at least three or four times the size of hers. She would have eventually found the tiny room, and my short, blonde resource room teacher would have been sitting there smiling across from a gorilla of a man. Limar stands almost at ceiling height and has the build of an NFL lineman. I picture him in the shorts and flip-flops he was accustomed to wearing during summer weightlifting, but even in a polo or a button-down he would have seemed to me unprofessional. It's something about his gum-chewing, his beady eyes, and his slicked greasy black hair. His face would have stretched briefly into a smile when my mom introduced herself. From there, they would have launched into a moderately friendly (she has a way of being fierce but never seeming impolite or out of control) but heated debate as to where I stood. He apparently told her quite frankly that he didn't know I was "classified."

He informed her, when she stressed my accommodations and asked politely for an extension on the assignment, that she wasn't doing me any favors.

"He's not gonna have accommodations in the real world. This is a college-level course, and he's going to have to rise to the standards of the class and not the other way around. Okay?"

After a certain point, when she realized she couldn't take anymore without flying off the handle, my mother would have backed down. I can see the leer with which he must have told my mother that he didn't think I was "getting" the class, confidently dumb, the same which he gave me when I, a sixteen-year-old autistic kid bested him at an explanation for an allegory I hadn't even yet read. I can imagine the sparks flying off of my mother's shoes as she marched down the hall and all five foot three of her aimed towards my guidance counselor.

She will even go to the principal with a full account of how she had been treated, and be assured that it was "utterly unacceptable." In the years to follow, Mom and I will find a lot of friends in teachers and guidance counselors who all have horror stories of dealing with Limar.

My anger won't last long. When on the first day of Global 10 I walk into my new class and see Cal, I already begin to ease up. My fears that my class would be painfully easy are realized. But as the year wears on and I begin to hear new incarnations of the familiar stories from my classmates who are ripping their hair out over obscene amounts of work, I find I don't envy them. I have Honors English and Spanish to satisfy my masochistic need for academic rigor, and I can now relegate math to its usual position as the bane of my existence.

Much later, when senior year comes to pass, Mom and I share stories.

"Guess what I heard on the announcements today? The principal congratulated our old friend Limar on his accomplishments as a football coach and inspiring teacher."

"Wow, and here I was all but assured he would be severely reprimanded. But you know what? I'm not surprised."

"Really? I sure as hell am."

"It's the same everywhere, Dylan. At my school all of the football players get breaks in class. There's the clique of the 'cool' teachers who happen to be the administrators' favorites, and they give everyone else a hard time. And there's the few, like Limar, who are full of themselves and can boss people around and it's okay. I love the kids I work with. Some are tough, but I love them. The really difficult part is dealing with the adults."

The once monumental problem of AP Euro is now little more than an unpleasant week fading into memory. I haven't regretted taking Global 10 or finishing IB US History in junior year only to decide to drop the advanced history the next year. These switches out of advanced classes won't impact my plans for college even marginally. I'm left to think of all of the stories Mom told me, all of the half-stories I've heard from the other room when she had friends over or spoke to them on the phone. All of the times Dad had complained that both his boss and the Social Security Department, right down to the software they were forced to use, were unreasonable. Essentially, it's all bullshit. Bullshit is pervasive. Bullshit politics, senseless red tape, insensitivity, and downright stubborn unreasonableness exist everywhere one can hope to find them, and certainly in most places one hopes never to find them. How I'm to survive is to be tenacious. Pick and fight my battles, but know when it isn't worth it. Plenty of times it's felt like I'm fighting the world. But sometimes circumstances and even the universe itself beg you to take the easier and more reasonable choice.

CHAPTER 18

WILD MAN

But just as there are those who don't understand my struggle, there are those who do. When I speak publicly about being autistic, I cite these misunderstandings as chief among the challenges associated with having a disability like mine. For every Mr. Limar or AP Euro I encountered, there was a class that made school worth it.

That class was Advanced English, and thank God I had it going into my years as an upperclassman. We picked apart not just *Lord of the Flies* and *Julius Caesar*, but Eugene O'Neil and Plath and Derek Walcott, and Walt Whitman. It gave me fuel as a writer, but most of all, it gave me another one of those anchors or home bases throughout the day where I felt safe: a forty-minute universe during which I was a force to be reckoned with. I wrote poems in response to Poe's "The City in the Sea" and Yeats' "The Second Coming," and to *One Hundred Years of Solitude*. By my standards today, the poems were wordy, vague, self-referential, and saturated with metaphors. I wrote about cadavers coming to life, dark forests, portents, demons, and dystopian dreamscapes built around the current war climate. Often, my poems were just images and metaphors clattered together in an attempt to solve some biblical question. But poems also gave me a chance to write about my own life in an appropriately veiled way, so that I could tease out my feelings without the vulnerability of fully revealing myself. Take for example this excerpt, appropriately melodramatic and drenched with emotion, about carrying the weight of unreciprocated feelings for a crush, which I wrote in study hall and showed my friend Jamie, the girl in question, sitting next to me.

The things I only wanted to say
locked in my soul as the parakeet,
in a triumphant yellow cage.

But where do I go?
to join the winter toads in their nowhereland of popsicle mud
with the helicopters
who bury themselves in the parched floor?

Even though I wasn't really invited to parties (aside from a basement concert here or there), I had advanced considerably in the social realm. Resisting my own trepidation about social media, I made a Myspace and a screen name. While social media eventually led to my reconnecting with Raven and represented a crucial step in integrating with the modern world, I still felt frozen (winter toads) by the gulf between the things I thought and expected from people and especially from myself, and reality. I was at the peak of my integration and awareness, which was both good and bad. It meant that I was a little bit less likely to put my foot in my mouth, but more likely to remember past indiscretions. If I wasn't hard on myself, if I kept making excuses like "it's because of my autism" how would I ever learn anything? If I didn't relentlessly try—to make a Myspace and, someday, a real, normal, honest-to-goodness social life complete with someone special—when would it ever happen? As much as I hated Limar's extreme and often misplaced weight-room axioms of motivation, I had to agree that failure was forgivable, but giving up was not an option. I had to try in earnest to bust out of the comfort bubble created by routine and my interests.

Raging and fiery behind a cool face
the northern winds in comparison
static...tropical.
And when memory visits me,
eyes softer than ever, smile warm
there, the tempest, buried within.

—*from a high school poem of mine entitled "Tempest"*

I was thankful for English, and for poetry (and for Karate, for Dad, for Cal, or any constant in my life) because junior year is the craziest year of high school by far. Along with the most rigorous academic demands including four college-level courses and their exams (one of which wasn't even in English) I was faced with the task of taking the SATs and looking for colleges that offered creative writing degrees. Then there was chorus. In the back of my mind I also knew I'd need to find someone to take to junior and senior prom. That's not even to mention the added weight of my cashier's and nursing home dining-room staff jobs that summer. The danger of course was that for an autistic person, especially a high-functioning one who has survived thus far largely by adhering to the rules, such stormy circumstances in the later years of high school (which are known to drive even the most well-prepared or adjusted teen to the brink of insanity) are a perfect breeding ground for wild, rebellious, impulsive behavior. Thankfully, I had the self-reflection afforded to me by the poems and short stories I wrote in my free time. Later on during junior year, when looking for a way for a version of my bizarre emotional suffering from the relationship with Raven to be taken seriously, I wrote a sixty-page novella about a reckless, nice guy-werewolf and his girlfriend, which was later read, thoroughly edited, and critiqued by a student teacher. Without writing, I'm quite unsure how I would have coped.

Similarly, the existentialist plays and stories we sometimes read in English—or rather the concept therein of an inherently meaningless life—had had an influence on me as a practical way of dealing with the world if only because it flew in the face of how I naturally wanted to see the things. When I dropped my books or discombobulated my papers, I wanted to believe in a mischievous force that railed against me. But in a world devoid of inherent meaning, I'm just clumsy. And that feels like a much more honest way of perceiving the world. But to anyone who isn't either enlightened or insane, a meaningless life is almost unbearable. So that's where writing came in.

SOME DEGREE OF ABANDON

This point in my life—post driver's license, pre-college—is where it gets tough explaining life with Asperger's. In my case, most of the major work of overcoming the sensory horrors of everyday life, as well as what had been the profound lack of coordination and social skills that make an autistic person stand out in a crowd, had already been completed. And this was huge. While I may not have had any idea who I was going to take to junior or real prom, I was sure that someday soon, when I seriously began dating, my disorder could be a second or even third date topic. But the step of making my disorder more and more invisible meant an entirely new set of challenges, including a tendency (both on my part and on the part of others) not to accept that my challenges were once so unique or profound.

People often tell me, when I describe the challenges of my condition, that they, too, have some of the same difficulties (with reading people, limited range of interests, oversensitivity to sensory stimuli, difficulty reading oneself, among others). And that's when I'll remind them that autism is a spectrum disorder for a reason. Wherever you stand on the spectrum, if you are autistic, chances are there is someone with a more minor and someone else with a more major set of challenges. This means that at the higher-functioning end of the spectrum, I am bound to have experiences highly relatable both to other higher-functioning autistic people and individuals who aren't clinically disabled at all—hence, my persistent issue of citizenship in two realms of existence.

Is social awkwardness exclusive to those on the spectrum? Absolutely not. Neither is pushing the boundaries of a parent's curfew or experimentation with substances. Neither is having a whirlwind relationship, or a first heartbreak. Rather these trials are widely experienced, and whosoever experiences them brings with them not only who they are, but their history. My otherwise ubiquitous challenges are uniquely exaggerated because of my status as someone with Asperger's.

It's normal, for instance, for teenagers to try to get drunk on the weekends. But in my case, the weight of so many watchful eyes on my life—for the sake of my safety and health, yadda yadda—had made me incredibly careful to remember the jacket I wore into school this morning, careful not to say the wrong thing, careful not to interrupt. I knew people who at seventeen already drove drunk and snuck into clubs, had multiple sexual partners, and did crazy things on the weekends while I was still sitting on the couch eating Friday night pizza and wings with the family. Not that I exactly wanted that for myself, but some degree of abandon was quickly becoming essential. In striving for normalcy, I'd somehow become one of the most polite, consequence-conscious and (I thought) consequentially uncool people I knew.

The seeds of my rebellion sprouted slowly. People say that autistic individuals have trouble getting perspective in their lives, but in my case my ability to gain multiple perspectives was an obstacle to my goals (one of which at that time was to know mischief). I had to work consciously against one of the people who I knew had my best interests at heart—my mom. Old habits die hard, and my mother was still intent on protecting me from dangerous situations, from friends who potentially weren't really friends, from my own lack of situational awareness and common sense. Negotiating and fighting for my freedom was a two-way street. Mom had to let the responsibility go and I had to learn how to handle it. And as you can imagine, while she wasn't happy about my drinking when she inevitably found me out, she did surprise me in other ways.

So far I'd gotten my mom to get me to go to two concerts—Sum 41 and Killswitch Engage—by myself, and recently, to Godsmack with Raven. We were speaking on the phone every night for progressively longer. We spoke of sexual fantasies and bizarre, hypothetical jokes. We laughed for at least fifteen minutes because my door creak had sounded like an elephant. I was attracted to Raven for real this time and for a number of reasons.

First of all, I liked her because she represented an intentional deviation from the norm. Raven's mischievous tendencies enticed me the same way my perceived innocence must have enticed her; she had a rebelliousness and independence I hoped would rub off on me. Second, she had seen me at my lamest and most vulnerable. The two years had been kind to both of us. Raven had blossomed and while she was pretty before, she was now gorgeous with a lip piercing and the experience of a serious relationship behind her. Since quitting football, I had taken to working out on my own and continued to lose weight. I was even growing a beard. So when I turned seventeen and had had my full license for a couple of months, and I asked Mom for the Odyssey, she surprised me by relenting with a half-joking remark about Raven attacking me in the back seat.

But for the most part, I began my mischief without her knowledge, with people who I knew my mother trusted.

FIRST TIMES

The first time I actually got drunk was a day after my first date. When I got to Cal's place, I wasted no time and spared no details of the night: the parked van, the Lamb of God music blaring, how she'd felt, how she'd looked. I left out the fact that this had been my first kiss. He shared my excitement in the way only a best friend really can, nodding so that his red hair shook everywhere.

Cal and I waited in his basement until his parents were sufficiently asleep. One corner of the basement was lined with cabinets. Cal teasingly opened one. They were lined with oblong and squat bottles and contained liquids in various shades of river water. He fished the bottle of Southern Comfort out from the bottom of the sink and handed it to me. He then groped in the back for a bottle of vodka and removed it with the precision of an alarm-scared jewel thief. I was nervous as hell.

We had our own private sampling party. The vodka was first, swallowed in championship speed from whiskey glasses. Next came the rum and then Southern Comfort. The SoCo set in and I sat back in a rotating chair, letting the room follow me around for a while. I sank deeper down and only when I felt the tension release, cold hands massaging me from inside, did I realize I'd been shaking. Why had I been so nervous? Cal put on an Usher song and shambled over to the cupboard.

"Hey, can you read this?"

I shook the chair off. Someone had weighted me down. I had a steering delay like a bad car. Cal, though half my size, had the advantage of being on his home turf, and he didn't look as drunk as I felt.

The bottle had two or three fingers' worth of canola-oil-colored stuff in it. The label was foreign, and I couldn't make out a word.

"Yeah, it says 'Some Italian Shit.'"

"Well, in that case." He glugged a mouthful. "Yup, definitely some Italian shit."

The liquor was sweet; the best out of any of them, but we knew we had to stop. The displaced and dirty bottles and glasses had stacked up around us.

When I was drunk enough, I called Raven as I'd promised. She took some strange vicarious pleasure watching me erode my innocence. I told her I wanted to see her. She listened to me chasing Cal around singing: "There's a Leprechaun in here and I'm gonna kill him!" Eventually, she had to go. It was late for anyone who wasn't messed up.

We ascended the cliff steps and washed everything out the best we could. Cal said he remembered where the bottles went, and I trusted him. It was hard to know if we'd done any visible damage to their collection. By my tally, we were at about eleven shots a piece. It was also hard to know if we were being quiet or not—I couldn't hear worth shit.

The next day, Cal slid me a couple of Excedrin on the sly, and I guess we thought we were golden. That spring and summer, my quiet reign of terror continued. Angelo and I got drunk whenever we could manage, which, much to our chagrin, wasn't often—getting Todd to pick up forty-ouncers for us from a gas station that he knew would serve him. Angelo or Cal came over and we attacked bottles. We had reckless, mostly harmless fun, and for a while, we didn't get caught.

But the pressure cooker that was junior year hadn't yet worn off, and after I gradually began to expect too much out of an emotionally turbulent relationship, Raven broke it off. To get into contact with and date Raven again, only to get my first kiss and argument and then break up within a month, was a cruel déjà vu. I felt, because of the relationship's brevity, and the immense egoic importance I'd placed upon the relationship, that the seriousness of my emotional reaction would be difficult for anyone else to understand. Of course, in retrospect, what then felt like the end of all things now seems not only quite surmountable but a necessary rite of passage. I'd never really experienced a bad night until after that.

OFF THE RAILS

Binghamton is the alcohol city. Of course, it's easy to think that as a seventeen-year-old, parked with his friends on the side of the road, drinking malt liquor. It doesn't just feel hopeless because I can fit all of my closest friends in a Toyota Corolla, that one of them is my recent ex-girlfriend, that we don't have anywhere better to go to drink. The whole place feels hopeless. The First Ward. The East Side. Down town. Just about anywhere, you aren't far from an abandoned factory (IBM, Endicott Johnson) and some alcoholic homeless. It feels, on nights like these, like the entire city is trying to lose the painful memories of its thriving days. Even the trees outside the window are bare of leaves and far from budding.

Beside me in the driver's seat, Angelo alternately takes mini-swigs from his bottle of Big Bear, using one huge thumb to text and swiveling around to talk to Raven.

"The answer is…NOOO!" he tells Raven with a smile and manner even the Joker might be afraid of.

"Stop! I'm gonna pee myself!" Raven is working on a forty-ounce Smirnoff Ice and has another waiting in the wings.

Most nights, Angelo and I are a two-man team. We speak in nonsense to each other, take manic pictures of both of us screaming at strangers; we like to think, and we have for years, that we're leaving our own weird mark on the world. Tonight, Angelo doesn't have to ask why I'm not saying much. It's all I can do to be in the car with Raven and act like everything's fine. I've even admitted to myself that we weren't a good couple, that our insecurities fed each other's, and that we'd stopped being able to tell each other how we feel.

I force myself into a chuckle and finish my first huge bottle.

"You better get going on that bottle before my goblin goes and drinks it. I've taught him tricks," I crack at Angelo, remembering I'm supposed to be having a good time.

He rolls his eyes and throws his head back, taking the Lord's name in vain and laughing.

"I'm driving tonight, remember?" but he takes a small swig anyway and Raven is laughing too. Abruptly, I get out of the car to piss, which switches the dome light on momentarily. Half an hour ago, I would have been sure that that brief flash of light had alerted the cop that must be lurking somewhere close and we'd be caught. But now, the cloud is coming over me and I'm beginning to care less.

Inside, Angelo and Raven are lamenting the weather and our lack of a proper drinking hole.

"It's a bit uncomfortable," Raven quips, "but whatevs."

"Well, I'm having a good time," Angelo says.

For a few minutes there, she'd just been the girl in the back seat. But now, something about her voice, something about the moonlight and her hair, brings it all back. She's again the girl who in the space of a couple months had seen past my weirdo and been the first girl to kiss me, to confide in me, and had given up on us. I think of everyone who has it bad for a friend of theirs, those who have serious crushes on teachers or on celebrities. The bitch of it is that knowing someone is unattainable makes not one bit of difference if you like her enough.

"Eh, looks like I gotta drink more 'cause I still care."

Later tonight, when we end up at Todd's friend Zach's house and I become too drunk to tolerate being around Raven without being with her, I make a critical error and storm out when no one's watching. I arrive home, having no recollection of the walk, a little after ten, when my mother is still awake. Here is where my memory of the night becomes fuzzy to non-existent.

"You've been drinking!" she yells incredulously. Laura is resurrected from a deep sleep and stands at the top of the steps, trying to corral the dogs, a haunted look on her face. Tomorrow, I will take my medicine and learn that my "little fuzzy" memory actually omits at least two hours' worth of night. Mom will force me to go to work at the old folks' home still a little tipsy, but all in all, thanks in part to my penchant for beating myself up, I'm fairly quickly forgiven. This is an important realization for my typically black-and-white brain, one I simultaneously wish I'd known as a fifth grader who was once mortified to get detention for forgetting his inhaler: namely, that I can make mistakes or even get in trouble without my life spiraling out of control.

FLAWED MACHINERY

So let me tell you a little bit about having autism and being a teenager. You want to drink and have a good time like everyone else, but even if you don't have the alcoholic genes that, courtesy of my grandparents, I do, you still have a sensory system that lies to you. The same faulty gastric mechanism that allows me to unflinchingly eat ten pieces of pizza allows me to drink just as many beers. I used to tell myself that I didn't believe alcohol would make me normal, not really, but sincerely hoped it might allow me to let loose. While the lack of inhibitions is nice, the social and situational awareness, which since its cultivation has largely been my saving grace, is greatly impacted by being drunk.

I want to be clear that I'm not saying that no one who's autistic should be able to have a drink. It's a personal choice, same as the routine you find suits you best and which you tend to follow. But I will say that I wasn't deterred the first time I got caught. Or the second time, or the third. Not until I was in college and had some hospitalizations for acute intoxication did I consider taking alcohol out of my life, which, without going into what is another story for another time, is where it currently stands. And that isn't because of the awkward situations I caused when, for instance, Laura had to pick me up from a kegger at Franky's, or cover for me when I got home late. It wasn't because of all of the white hairs my college hospital visits caused my loved ones, or the rifts it put between me and my friends. I didn't even quit because it never helped me with women or to look cool. The simple fact is I was never able to cultivate an awareness capable of keeping me out of harm's way when I drank.

But with my fires of loss from the failed relationship with Raven cooling, with my new jobs starting and with junior prom officially over, some of the stressors in my life were turning to motivators. Not that I wasn't still nervous about where I'd end up (just because one of Cal's friends had agreed to go to junior prom with me didn't mean I had a date for real prom; just because I'd done well in all of my classes didn't mean I'd necessarily come out of high school with flying colors); but I no longer felt completely overwhelmed by life. I could organize without flipping out. I gave up on caring about people who didn't make half an effort to understand me. Only earlier this year, when I asked my former square-dancing partner to junior prom and she'd promptly laughed in my face, I'd simply looked elsewhere. I wasn't quite up to the realization that life wasn't perfect and that my standards for myself were absurdly high, but I was on the right track.

CHAPTER 19

SETTLING IN,
MOVING ON

Stay in one place long enough, and it will start to feel like home. By the time senior year came around, I felt as if I and the rest of the class of 2008 had finally grown into the place. Classmates of mine were now the faces of the student government organizations and the presidents of clubs. We swung lanyards attached to car keys and escaped the building every chance we got. Those of us who hadn't bought into the Full IB curriculum, which necessitated one thousand hours of community service and a gigundo research paper, congratulated ourselves on the one or two extra free periods we had earned every day. The officers and monitors knew us by name. The guy who checked my bag every morning now only gave it a pat as I walked by. We had inherited the kingdom and all of the rights that went with it, and we were about to be kicked out.

Nothing made me realize how far I'd come more than watching Laura jump through all of the same hoops I'd jumped through in years past. Poor Laura had not dodged the AP Euro bullet, and there were times even during junior year when she'd spend several more hours on homework than I did. Last year around the time I dated Raven, Laura began going out with Joey, and they had stayed together. I watched and listened as they went through the ups and downs of being attached to one another, as they re-fell in love and almost broke up. One part of me wondered what she understood about relationships that I didn't. But I also realized for the first time, the way only someone learning something vicariously is able, what a pain in the ass being in a relationship truly is. Maybe relationships were like AP Euro. There were those of us who for one reason or another couldn't be bothered with it for more than a week. Out of those who stayed, some (like Laura) said it was an aggravating waste of time, and others seemed perfectly at home spending every evening devoted to another entity (be it a person or a textbook). Most people really appeared better for having gone through the struggle, though. It was just a question of which struggles were meant for us, how we dealt with them.

Laura and I in a lot of ways are opposites and deal with conflict quite differently. She despises reading, and I love it. She likes economics and math. Laura is very good at arguing a point; I tend to avoid conflict. I can get up in front of an audience and speak or sing or what have you, and in fact, my senior year I decided to do much more of just that. While shyer than me, Laura has infinitely more naturally-occurring people skills than I do. And it's for that reason, coupled with the fact that recently she'd been covering for me in my mischief, that I really consider Laura to be an older sister and role model for me. Being able to give her advice on her Spanish homework or English paper made me feel a bit more like an older brother again, as if there were some definitive and tangible help I could give.

But there were still plenty of pressures swirling around me like chariots on a battlefield. IB exams and prom awaited at the end of the year. But for the first part of the year, college applications were everyone's headache. Now, just when I was arguably getting used to where I was, I was asked to orchestrate my biggest and most improbable life change yet. And for someone with Asperger's, the topic of college can be a touchy one to broach. The first and most obvious question is: am I capable? I got the distinct feeling that I was Icarus and my independence was the sun. I had to be very practical and careful about doing this. If I chose wisely, it would mean admittance into a setting where the standards influencing the norm would change to better accommodate my eccentricities and to shrink the significance of my boundary-straddling life outlook. At college, so many others would be more strange and reclusive than I had grown to be, so that where I belonged and who knew about my diagnosis might finally be my own decision.

A PREVIEW OF COLLEGE

The road stretches out in front of us—Mom's behind the wheel, and I'm trying to let the scenery fill my mind for a second before I get preoccupied with the nature of the trip. It's one of those highways in upstate New York that gets interrupted by traffic lights and small towns. Somewhere, not too much farther down the road, in Hamilton, New York, is Colgate University, one of the four schools I'm choosing to apply to (all of which are in upstate New York). This will be my first visit. And though by this time, as it is likely the last college visit I'll have, the college discussion is starting to feel a bit worn out, we're having the discussion again.

"I was meeting with a representative from Colgate not too long ago. Someone came to my school. And they said that the way Colgate recruits is that they set all of the applicants from each school up against each other. Which means that everyone who did Full IB will get ahead of me."

There's a pause while the GPS yet again updates our route, giving more redundant directions.

"It's ridiculous. As if I don't already have enough to worry about, I need to wonder how many Full IB applicants they're going to have."

"Well, we've been over this. Your application is almost done, isn't it?"

"Yeah, just about."

"Okay. So let me ask you this. Assuming we get there and you don't hate it—which you may, we may pull up on campus and you might decide within two minutes that you hate it. You might decide that you love it and that you'll do everything you can to get there. But assuming you don't hate it right off the bat, what do you have to lose?"

"Yeah, I guess." She's right, of course. It's the same as they'll tell me when I do go to college; for the first draft (of an essay or application, or what have you), you silence the critic. If I constantly bring into question the quality or futility of the application, I won't get anything done.

"Dylan, that's why we're doing this. It isn't like Colgate is a million miles away, it's practically in our backyard. Besides, I think you have a really great shot. I think you made a great decision bringing up your disability in your college essay, and I think that's actually a major selling point for you."

I have the same hope, but some of the old stigmas are fresh in my mind. What if they don't find my diversity appealing? What if, as I once had, they saw my autism more as a risk and a detriment?

All of the colleges, with the exception of Geneseo, which is a little over three hours away, are pretty much in my backyard. Part of growing up, I guess, is a marriage of following and paring down your dreams. Would I like to think that I could thrive at UC Berkeley or Arizona or Mississippi? Most definitely. But what would happen if one day I woke up completely overwhelmed with life and a thousand miles away from anyone who truly understood me? What if I woke up in a hospital or jail cell after one of my black-out episodes? How would my family pay for airline tickets to such places at just a moment's notice? The road held no answers, just farm houses and little thickets. So in addition to colleges that offered a writing major but didn't have the stressors of an Ivy League school, I picked colleges a reasonable distance from home.

When we do make it to campus, we've entered a world of rolling, tree-lined hills interspersed with brick buildings. Though it's mostly deserted, the people I do see are wrapped in Cashmere sweaters, making their way to luxury German sedans waiting like sleeping dogs in the parking lots.

"Well, it is really pretty here," I tell Mom when we're almost back to the car and she asks my overall impression. I'm not really sure beyond that.

"My friend Allison went here, and she really liked it. Did really well too. She told me that she used to sit at the bar almost every afternoon, you know, back when they had bars on campuses, and people used to think she was one of the slackers. But she'd get all of her work done first and she graduated at the top of her class."

"Well that would be nice." I try to imagine myself at Colgate, or at Ithaca or Geneseo battling the wind, scurrying between the buildings, head down, buzzing with all of my commitments and parties and beautiful, down-to-earth, intelligent women. The image has all of the daydreamish, ambiguous qualities of a fantasy, but doesn't feel all that far off.

"Dylan, I'm so proud of you. To think where you were just a few years ago. And now look at you; you're going to be a man of the world. I thought we'd take a ride around Hamilton and then head back, what do you say?"

I have nothing against small towns, but Hamilton is extremely small. I can't imagine there will be any sort of music or club scene.

"Well, this is quaint."

"Yeah, it's a small college town. And it may suit you, it may not. What do you say, should we head back?"

The sun is giving an orangeish tinge to the darkening sky. Yes, it's time to go. Mom pulls in a gas station.

"Do you want to drive?"

It's going to be quite some time before I say no to that question. Driving will retain its novelty to me for some time. I catch a look at myself in the mirror and have one of those revelatory thoughts that just sort of jumps down on you one day. One day, I'm in eighth grade with peach fuzz, picking out my first electric razor, and the next, I'm mostly through high school. I look in the mirror and have the makings of a full beard.

"Who would have thought I'd be good at driving?"

"Not in a million years."

But I am good at it. And I think that (when Mom's not in the car) the intensity of the speed calms me the same way heavy metal does. For someone who has trouble seeing the trees for the forest, who sees hours of arduous homework instead of three manageable half-hour assignments, driving forces me into the present moment—no winding thought tangents, no horizon full of dizzying possibilities, just the road in front of me, quite manageable. Just my foot on the gas, and the next couple of miles in front of me.

ON STAGE

With Karate sufficiently in the rear-view of my life and with most of my applications sent in, my schedule had a bit more breathing room. I'd recently taken a theater class and thought it might be worthwhile to try and jump to the other side of the creative process. So I auditioned for *To Kill a Mockingbird*, Binghamton High's fall play in 2007. I wasn't entirely surprised to have been given a semi-leading role, the part of Sheriff Heck Tate. Even though I was no longer a full head taller than the rest of my classmates, I was no small guy. I thought it was good casting, especially since my director, Mr. Largo, said I could keep my beard. Even with my family and several friends always insisting I should go into acting, I always wondered how well my penchant for impersonations would translate to the stage. I'd have a lot to work on when it came to bodily awareness.

I was surprised to find the whole process rather enjoyable. I didn't have too many scenes and found I got along well with everyone, especially the underclassmen who had no way of knowing my reputation or diagnosis. One of my newfound friends was a freshman named Josh who somehow knew more about metal than I did, and shared my bizarre sense of humor. We sat in the audience trading random phrases, watching Henry, the high-functioning autistic kid cast as Boo Radley, grapple with our Bob Ewell, or the pretty young Camille practicing her breakdown as she learns of her husband Tom Robinson's death.

"Archibald's Cactus Committee," I whispered.

"Charity banjo snatching," he retorted.

"Cream cheese apocalypse."

We could go for hours, and we often did. I'm struck in retrospect how much my mindset had changed. I didn't care that Shana, or my fellow seniors starring in the play, would see me hanging with freshmen, or overhear me talking about all sorts of assorted nonsense.

By the time spring rolled around, I started to hear back from colleges. And while I'd like to say that I had the pick of the litter, the decision really came down to financial aid. The state schools had gladly accepted me, but gave minimal assistance. Colgate put me on a waiting list, which I was strangely fine with, having realized that Colgate's demographic was quite homogeneous, with its potentially stifling academic pressure. Ithaca College, on the other hand, a school I was at first reluctant to apply to since we'd visited its comparatively modest campus directly after Cornell's magnificent monstrosity, seemed my best bet. Not only did they have an office for students with disabilities, they also had a reputation for being eclectic. Even so, my decision was far from a no-brainer. It involved a lot of discussion and hair-pulling. But eventually, it was decided. I visited one more time and picked up some IC shirts just in time for spring.

I'd found acting to be so much fun that when the time came, I auditioned for the musical, *Cabaret,* in the spring, and landed another leading role, this time as suave smuggler and Nazi party member Ernst Ludwig. Of course, I'd wanted the starring role as Cliff, but so did everyone auditioning. Another lead role would be quite a way to end my school career. Though *Cabaret* was somewhat more demanding, the familiar faces, of which Camille, playing the lead Sally Bowles, was one, made it a sweet proposition. The show came together slowly, and not without plenty of stress. Those of us who caught the brunt of Largo's wrath joked that if he'd had hair in the first place, it would all be gone by now. The flirtatious atmosphere that the show created was also perfect for me, as I still scrambled to find a prom date. Before I knew it, dress rehearsals were around the corner.

Stepping into the clean, yellow light of the hall from the dusty velvet of backstage usually felt like a letdown to me. It wasn't that I missed the stage, or being told by my director's sharpening voice that I should know my blocking by now, or wondering, almost continuously, if the timing on my entrances was off, if my German accent was on, how much work I needed until my suave Nazi smuggler was believable. Nevertheless, there's a restless comfort in the wings of a stage, a clandestine pride that comes with being just out of sight but not out of earshot. You could catch people changing in the wings if your timing was right (or wrong, as the case might be), and that was wrapped up in that weird transitional beauty of those quick ten feet, too.

But today was a semi-dress rehearsal, and in the hallway, commotion. Gary, an eighth grader wearing braces and a blue sailor suit bounced a vending machine rubber ball. The ball skipped and his hand missed it, but Gary stood still for a second, dribbling at the air. I followed his gaze to see Camille farther down the hall in front of a dressing rack. Her back a creamy coffee color, was bare, and when she turned around, her forearm and a couple of layers of duct tape were the only things keeping her from full exposure. We both stood transfixed for a second before I snapped out of it.

"Have some respect, man," I said, and with an arm around Gary, made to evacuate the hallway, but not before Camille caught my eye, a smile sparkling on her face.

The next morning, I woke up with an excruciating backache. A doctor's visit and two missed days of work later, I was nursing two herniated discs. Previously, I had had no idea what an injury could do in terms of exposure to female attention. If I felt like I was pulling double duty before, that is, being an oddball with Angelo and the guys, and trying to be smooth in public and with girls, that feeling went doubly now. My co-stars gave me back massages, asked me if I was alright. It turned out all of the coping mechanisms I'd been developing to help me in my everyday life translated relatively well to acting, which in turn, finally gave me some ease with which to approach girls.

One day, Camille came up to me with a smile that was somehow bashful and confident.

"Let's exchange numbers so that I can keep track of you, make sure you're healing up alright." She had a voice like melting butter, and it made me feel good all over.

"Sure, absolutely." I fiddled with my pocket and prayed my phone wouldn't choose now to die or malfunction. Now, after college and grad school and some serious relationships, I would have picked out the intention in her sentence. At the time, I wasn't sure where any of this was headed. All I knew was that I was glad someone was interested in me.

We began talking on the phone as Raven and I once had. I could talk to her for hours, and we would laugh like loons, especially if I had snuck some liquor or she had snuck some wine. In the safe, dark confines of our respective rooms, I opened up to her about my problems, about being a socially awkward senior, about not having a date to prom, and she opened up to me about hers, about the stresses of being an overachiever and people pleaser (her schedule made mine look like a vacation itinerary). For some reason I still don't quite understand, it was infinitely easier for me to get to know someone, to put my best foot forward, over the phone. I really understood what Angelo had meant when he said he had a much easier time online. Something about that distance, about being one step removed, felt much more natural to me (perhaps because of the gradually shrinking gulf in understanding between others and myself).

With prom drawing nearer, a lot of my old fears started to return. What would it mean for my social standing if I went to prom by myself? What would it mean for my self-esteem, to throw myself at a goal for four whole years only to be denied at the end? Raven had a boyfriend, so she was out of contention. My friend Brooke had very gently let me down for a junior prom request and now she, too, was taken. Maybe my fears during the years with Mr. Noel had been justified. Maybe my reputation among my own class was too ruined for anyone to find me attractive enough for a prom date, no matter how much I'd progressed or how much weight I'd lost (and I was down at least fifty pounds from the start of sophomore year). I'd been toying with the idea of asking someone in sophomore or junior year, but I was also uncertain of what that would mean for my image.

Camille and I had begun meeting in the hall between periods on the way to our respective classes, and maybe it was what she was wearing that day, or the way she said, "Oh, I'm sure you'll find someone," that finally shot the big bulb off in my head. For the rest of the day, I tried to find a suitable means of asking Camille if she'd go with me. With time, I felt, running out, I settled on a simple text message, to which she responded enthusiastically.

I had lead in both a play and a musical. I was going to graduate in the top twenty-five of my class of over three hundred fifty, and now I had a prom date. I still had no idea how I was going to negotiate the move away from home, or if a writing degree was even practical.

ON A LIFE WITH AUTISM

At the end of our presentations on living with autism, Mom and I pull up a picture of me in my prom tux, black with lavender vest and tie to match Camille's purple dress. I tell the story of how I decided it would be a good idea to get to know my prom date a little better, how in a very short period of time we went on a date and became a couple. I really did enjoy my prom, and sweating there on the dance floor pressed closely against my date, I felt bad for everyone just sitting around, who decided dancing wasn't fun or for them. I tell them that, true to the way of the world, even though we knew I'd be leaving for Ithaca in the fall and Camille would have to finish up her diploma, and the relationship likely wouldn't survive, we couldn't help becoming an official couple. It grew into the most serious relationship I'd have until well into college.

On the way back through my story to the present day, Mom and I enumerate all of my challenges, forcing our audience and ourselves to remember a time when I couldn't hold a fork straight, didn't talk about anything except Batman and the Beach Boys, and didn't much want friends or know the first thing about attaining them. I tell them that my one-time occupational therapist became a close family friend and my confirmation sponsor, and was the only person in attendance at my graduation who had as much a right as my parents to shower me with praises of how proud she was. I pride myself in being humble; I'm not usually fond of people who consider themselves to be the hero of their own story. But this is one time I allow myself to exude pride, especially if by so doing, I can convince parents and teachers and other autistic kids themselves that their efforts, including working through cafeteria meltdowns and shattered self-standards, are heroically important.

I spent a lot of time, as did everyone who worked with me, trying to peel back all of the confining layers of my autism, trying to connect myself to the outside world, to adapt to the point where I'd be unrecognizable from anyone neuro-normative. I can say that though I've accomplished a lot of my goals, I've yet to get there, and I'm not sure I really want to. Though I may always take a second longer to discern whether someone is being serious or sarcastic; though I'll never be comfortable in bright sunlight or in the midst of multiple conversations; though I may have to (due to a faulty sensory system) constantly wonder whether or not I should feel full or hungry—I've stopped wanting to be someone that I'm not. I've stopped wanting to be better than myself. It was sometime during those last years of high school that I realized how silly it seemed that I should ever seriously want to be the popular kid, how fortunate I was to be able to function so well in the shared realm and to have my few good friends.

I wouldn't be the same writer or the same compassionate person without my autism. I've reached a point where having autism works for me just as much as it works against me, and though it may not be a technically true sentiment, I don't consider myself to have a disorder, per se. I make sure my audience knows that I wouldn't trade a normal or easier childhood for the story I have to tell.

I scan the audience for families sitting with children buried in Game Boys or books or phones, with their heads tilted up into the corners of their room, the ethereal depths of their minds. I promise the parents and caregivers in the audience the only thing I really can guarantee based on my own experience. And this is that in the end, all of the hard work pays off and that these amazing little individuals in their lives will surprise them, probably beyond their wildest expectations.

REFERENCES

Asperger, Hans (1944) "'Autistic Psychopathy' in Childhood" (trans. and annot. U. Frith) in *Autism and Asperger Syndrome* (1991) Uta Frith (ed.) Cambridge University Press, Cambridge. pp.37, 39, 42.

Frith, Uta (1991) "Asperger and his Syndrome" in *Autism and Asperger Syndrome,* Uta Frith (ed.) Cambridge University Press, Cambridge. pp.10–12.

Wing, Lorna (1991) "The Relationship Between Asperger's Syndrome and Kanner Autism" in *Autism and Asperger Syndrome,* Uta Frith (ed.) Cambridge University Press. Cambridge, p.77.